MW01518537

BEHIND
CLOSED
DOORS

BEHIND CLOSED DOORS

Christians, Pornography, and the Temptations of Cyberspace

ROBERT J. BAIRD, M.DIV., MSW, PH.D.
RONALD L. VANDERBECK, PSY.D.

THE HOPE AND RECOVERY INSTITUTE

PUBLISHER'S NOTE: This book is intended for general information only and is not intended to supplant advice, diagnosis, treatment, or therapy by a personal physician or professional counselor.

Published in Hudsonville, Michigan by Tribinium Corporation.

Printed in the United States of America.

ISBN-13:   978-0-9799456-0-1

Contents

"Here I am! I stand at the door and knock."

REVELATION 3:20, NIV

An Invitation to Renewal and Restoration

Tim's wife had only been gone for a minute or so. As usual he had given her a peck on the cheek, wished her a good day, and waved goodbye. He waited until she had pulled her car out of the driveway before he booted up his computer. Ever since he'd gotten his new computer he looked forward to her leaving for work. It's not that he didn't love her; he truly did. But this was time for him to do something he wouldn't conceive of doing when she was at home. He closed the door to the den and removed from his chair the notes he had brought home from last night's Bible study. It didn't take him long to get comfortable and to find what he was looking for. He had his favorite sites. Within moments he was so immersed in what he was doing that he never heard the door open. His heartbroken wife stood speechless.

John graduated toward the top of his class in law school and was quickly recruited by a prestigious firm. With a private office, personal secretary, and law clerks to assist him, he was given all the resources to be a successful attorney. However, the senior partners could not understand why his billings were so low. He always arrived early and was one of the last to leave. But John wasn't working on briefs when he was behind the closed doors of his office.

Kate considered herself a typical soccer mom. Her husband had a good paying job, so she didn't have to work. She had three kids whom she would cart around to school and sporting events. By all appearances she seemed to have the perfect life. Nice husband. Great kids. Big house. But Kate was bored. Her husband spent so many hours at work that she didn't feel her needs were being met. So Kate turned to Internet chatrooms. She wasn't looking primarily for sex. What she craved was affirmation and affection. There, she found the attention she sought.

Stephen was a sophomore in high school. His parents took him to see a psychologist who specializes in adolescent depression. And for sure, Stephen presented with all the telltale signs of depression. He was sleeping through all of his classes at school. He was no longer hanging out with his friends. He used to be an avid soccer player, but not any more. Clinically speaking, he was depressed. But what his parents didn't know was that after they went to bed at night, Stephen would quietly boot up his computer and surf through porn sites till the wee hours of the morning.

Jill was in middle school—eighth grade, to be exact. When her parents came to the offices of The Hope and Recovery Institute, both their faces were ashen. Her father's hands trembled as he described their discovery of pictures on their daughter's digital camera, pictures of Jill and her boyfriend. They had met in their church's youth group. What should have been a story of puppy love instead escalated to become a story of coercion. The boyfriend had introduced Jill to the world of "virtual" reality, where reality quickly becomes distorted. Jill truly believed that what she encountered there represented normal relationships. But she had nothing to base her conclusion on since sex was never openly discussed in her home.

If any of these stories sounds familiar to you, it's not surprising. Statistics show that one in five Americans uses the Internet to look for pornography or engage in cybersexual "chat." In fact, sex is the most frequently searched topic on the Internet—more than games, music, travel, jokes, cars, jobs, weather, and health material *combined*.[1] In a recent survey, one in ten people reported believing he or she was addicted to sex via the Internet. Moreover, one in four disclosed feeling that on at least one occasion his or her online sexual behavior was out of control.[2]

Focus on the Family conducted a survey with Zogby International indicating that one out of five American adults may have looked for sex on the Internet. Twenty percent of the respondents admitted to having visited a sexually oriented website (representing approximately 40 million adults). In this survey nearly 26 percent of men and nearly 17 percent of women indicated that it was either somewhat or very likely that the Internet is capable of providing sexual fulfillment. Not sexual stimulation. Sexual fulfillment.[3]

Rabbit Hunting and the Proliferation of Porn

In 1953 an event took place that would forever change the moral complexion of American society: the publication of *Playboy* magazine. With his bunny insignia and Playboy Playmates, Hugh Hefner introduced pornography into mainstream American culture. What before had been shunned or ridiculed was soon to become not only tolerated but also celebrated. Prior to *Playboy*, the public perception was that users of porn were perverted or twisted. But Hefner marketed his material in such a way that his readers could consider themselves sophisticated, intelligent, and debonair. In a very real way pornography became fashionable. No longer hidden in back alleys, pornography became readily available at newsstands and delivered by the U.S. Postal Service.

The popularity of Hefner's product was enormous, and for nearly fifteen years Playboy Enterprises monopolized the market. Then, in 1969, an advertisement appeared in the *New York Times*. It featured *Playboy*'s bunny logo centered in a rifle sight accompanied by the caption, "We're going rabbit hunting." The ad went on to read, "If you can catch a rabbit once you can catch him again. That's what we did in Germany and France. The U.S. market will be the next to fall. We are going to catch this rabbit in his own backyard. We are the magazine that gives men what they are looking for."

And so began the pornography wars. *Penthouse* declared a full offensive in attempt to dominate the market. In 1974 Larry Flynt joined the fray, launching *Hustler* magazine. As these publishers pressed to achieve a larger share of the market, they pushed the envelope of acceptability. In a short period of time, the images depicted in these magazines changed from erotica to full frontal nudity. Over the next twenty years, content of these publications would include ever-increasingly hardcore sexual depictions.

The technology of the 1970s and 1980s then catapulted pornography into a multi-billion dollar industry. Cable and satellite TV permitted viewers to access pornography from the privacy of their homes. No longer was there a risk of being seen purchasing a dirty magazine. Behind closed doors Americans were beginning to do in private what they never would have considered doing in public.

The introduction of VHS tapes and inexpensive videocassette players magnified the problem. By 1992, Americans had bought or rented 405 million adult videos, generating $1.6 billion in profits for the pornography industry. By 1999 the revenues for video pornography increased to $4.05 billion. And by 2006, 957 million adult videos and DVDs were sold, generating $3.62 billion in pornography revenues.[4] What happened next, though, makes these statistics seem miniscule by comparison.

The introduction of the Internet in the 1990s granted anyone with a personal computer and Internet connection access to pornography twenty-four hours a day, seven days a week. With little to no restrictions, people of all ages now have access to a vast smorgasbord of smut. All it takes is the click of a mouse to view all sorts of images, from the erotic and titillating to the downright bizarre.

The Reality of Internet Pornography

- The pornography industry generates $12 billion dollars in annual revenue - larger than the combined annual revenues of ABC, NBC, and CBS. Of that, the Internet pornography industry generates $2.5 billion dollars in annual revenue.

- 87% of university students polled have virtual sex mainly using Instant Messenger, webcam, and telephone.

- According to comScore Media Metrix, Internet users viewed over 15 billion pages of adult content in August 2005.

- According to the National Center for Missing and Exploited Children (NCMEC), child pornography reports increased 39% in 2004. More than 20,000 images of child pornography are posted on the Internet every week.

- In 2005, worldwide revenue from mobile phone pornography is expected to rise to $1 billion and could grow to three times that number or more within a few years.

- One in five children who use computer chatrooms has been approached over the Internet by pedophiles.

- Nine out of 10 children aged between eight and 16 have viewed pornography on the Internet. In most cases, the sex sites were accessed unintentionally when a child, often in the process of doing homework, used a seemingly innocent sounding word to search for information or pictures.

- Sex is the #1 searched for topic on the internet.

- 60% of all website visits are sexual in nature.

- 41% of women said they had deliberately viewed or downloaded pornographic pictures and movies.

- 51% of pastors say cyberporn is a possible temptation. 37% say it is a current struggle. 4 in 10 pastors have visited a porn site.

Data provided by Enough Is Enough[5]

An Invitation
to Renewal and Restoration

No question about it, an astonishing number of people within the faith community struggle with sexual sin on the Internet. And it is for them, their spouses, and others who want to help them that this book is written. This book, however, is not just about calling attention to a problem. This book is about solutions. With inspiration from Scripture and insight from the behavioral sciences, this book presents specific and practical interventions to assist those struggling with sexual sin stemming from the Internet. The purpose of this book is to liberate people from sexual sin not only by educating them to the risks and destructive power of cybersexual behavior, but also to provide the tools and strategies essential for life-changing renewal and transformation.

The format of this book is essentially the same for each chapter. Beginning with personal stories based on the experiences of those who sought treatment at the Hope and Recovery Institute, each chapter then provides an analysis of the situation as well as encouraging biblical references intended to inspire hope. Most importantly readers will find practical strategies designed to help renew and restore a healthy, Christian sexuality.

Our hope is that you'll discover the solution to recovery is a renewed relationship with God. Throughout these chapters may his gentle call inspire changed thoughts and behaviors and a new way of living as followers of Christ.

Sexual struggles are not new. As accounted for in the Bible, humanity has struggled with sexual issues throughout the ages. Joseph encountered sexual temptation when Potiphar's wife tried to seduce him (Gen.39:7-19). Sexual gluttony contributed to the destruction of Sodom and Gomorrah (Gen.18:16-33). Lot and his two daughters had an incestuous relationship (Gen. 19:30-38). Abraham believed his wife was incapable of conceiving a child, so he chose to have an adulterous relationship with Hagar (Gen. 16:1-16). Believing she was a prostitute, Judah slept with his daughter-in-law (Gen. 38). Sexual manipulation is implied in the story of Samson and Delilah (Judg. 16). The King of Israel, David, abused his power in order to have an adulterous affair with Bathsheba (2 Sam. 11-12). David's third son, Absalom, rebelled against his father and made it public knowledge that he had sexual relations with all of his father's wives (2 Sam. 18:6-15).

Warnings against adultery are specified in Prov. 6:20-29. The destructiveness of adultery is addressed, metaphorically, in the *Allegory of Unfaithful Jerusalem* (Ezek. 16). In his letter to the church in Rome, the Apostle Paul addressed the multiplicity of ways in which people rebel against a covenant relationship with God, including sexual immorality. Similar admonitions appear in another letter penned by Paul, this one to the church located in one of the largest seaports—Corinth—in the Roman Empire, a city renowned for sexual excesses and immorality. In 1 Corinthians 5, Paul insists that such practices not be tolerated in the church.

The Bible, in many ways, is a book about relationships. The Bible is about people's relationship with God and with each other. What is remarkable about the stories contained in the Bible is how real they are. As a book that serves as the foundation of an entire faith system, it's remarkable how genuine and authentic these stories are. The superheroes of our faith, our Biblical ancestors, had problems similar to ours. Like Christians in the twenty-first century, they struggled with temptation. Like Christians whose lives are surrounded by a secular, sexualized culture, they too made bad choices.

But the stories in the Bible are also stories of redemption. And so are the stories you are about to read in this book. These are stories of people from the faith community who experienced the dark, chaotic forces of cyberspace. As clients who sought treatment at the Hope and Recovery Institute, they have agreed to share their stories. Only names and other identifying information have been changed to protect their privacy.

One of their stories may be your story. Our prayer is that, by the grace of God, you too will accept God's invitation to renewal and restoration.

2

"I Was Just Curious"

The Temptations of Internet Pornography

DAVE'S STORY

My name is Dave. For about three years, though, I might as well have been known as Dr. Jekyll or Mr. Hyde. I lived a secret life that was known only to me, a surreptitious existence contaminated by pornography.

Nobody knew about my dark side until the week after my wife threw a surprise birthday party to celebrate my fortieth birthday. She had invited practically everyone and anyone we had ever known. Family, my parents, friends, the pastor, and even my boss were invited. She and the kids put together a PowerPoint presentation detailing my life's journey. Most of it was humorous, but there were some photographs that served as a stark reminder of who I had been and what I had become.

After the presentation, there were speeches. My eldest son talked about me being the coach for just about every team sport my kids ever played. He poked fun at me, suggesting that I had wanted to relive my childhood (which was probably true). He talked about me always being at his teacher conferences and about the time when he was in the sixth grade school play and I cancelled a business trip just to be there. He mentioned how I was always pestering him and his brother and sister to do their homework and joked about "dad's alarm clock" that seemed to go off at the same time each night when I would make them go to their rooms to do their homework. Little did he know that I would send them off to their rooms so I could do some "work" of my own on the computer. My best friend gave a little speech poking fun at my receding hairline. His gift to me was a pair of bifocal reading glasses and some hair dye to cover up the gray. In his speech he talked about how he has never seen me lose my temper (except when the Yankees lost the World Series to the Diamondbacks). He called me a "family man" and praised me for my love and devotion to my wife and kids.

Later that night my wife commented that she thought it was sweet that I began blushing while he was speaking. What she didn't know was that the truth of what I'd been doing online made me feel like anything *but* a devoted husband and father. Following my best friend, my pastor spoke of my commitment to the church and my willingness to teach Sunday school and open our home for Bible study. It is true; for the past ten years I have volunteered to teach Sunday school. It's also true that for years my wife and I have hosted numerous Bible studies in our home. But what he didn't know— what no one knew— was that the same computer I used to write material for Christian education was also used to surf the World Wide Web for pornography.

The showering of praise and attention at my birthday party was more than I could bear. Later that night, after everyone was gone and my wife and I were lying in bed, I prayed and started to cry. I'm not a touchy-feely type of guy, and so tears are not typical for me, but the experience from that night cut me to the core. I realized I was no longer the person I wanted to be. I realized I was no longer the person I knew my wife wanted me to be. I realized I was no longer the man that Christ called me to be.

It took me a week to muster up the courage to talk to my wife, but I had to. I had to tell her what was going on and that I needed to make a radical change to get my life back in order.

I told her (just as I'm telling you) that pornography has not always been a problem for me. It was only over the span of three years that my life was turned upside-down because of that stuff. Back when I was a teenager as well as in college, I would occasionally look at my friends' *Playboy* magazines, but it was never something I did on a regular basis. I never bought a magazine or rented a video. Until the Internet came along, pornography had never been a problem.

For me, my troubles started out of curiosity.

We first connected to the Internet in the early '90s. At that time my motivation (and I say this with all sincerity) was good. I wanted my children to benefit educationally. The World Wide Web had so many positive benefits. The kids could do research for their home-work, and my wife and I could email family and friends at any time. It was relatively cheap and fast. Since my parents were aging and strug-gling with health problems, I could use the Internet to find informa-tion on healthcare. It was fascinating how quickly I could find just about anything I wanted simply by clicking the mouse and typing in a few key words.

To say that my first encounter with Internet pornography was acci-dental would be a lie. I knew exactly what I was doing. I didn't know, though, what I was getting myself into. It was late at night and my wife and kids were in bed asleep. I turned the computer screen to the side, just in case my wife should walk in. I had heard all the talk about Internet porn and was curious to see what it was all about. That night, after connecting to the Internet, I typed in four letters: p-o-r-n. Within moments of hitting the Enter key, I had a long list of Web sites offering me an unimaginable array of choices. I hesitated for a moment— but no longer. I knew I shouldn't be doing it, but I clicked the mouse any-way. In that moment, my life took an unexpected turn.

What was I doing? I never was the kind of person who would go to stores and buy porn. That just seemed wrong and, besides, I'd rather die than be seen going into an adult bookstore! But here I was, on the Internet looking at porn sites. It was so private and secret. No one knew what I was doing, and there was so much to see. As

I surfed around, I wondered where on earth they found all of those attractive women to pose like that.

My first experience lasted about an hour that night, until the family dog walked into the room. I didn't even know she was there until she nudged the back of my chair. I nearly had a heart attack thinking it was my wife or one of the kids. I remember yanking the power cord right out of the wall. Startled by the dog, I momentarily came to my senses. In that moment, a wave of shame washed over me. What I'd been doing was wrong, and I knew it. The next morning my wife sensed that something was up, but I didn't dare tell her what I'd done. I promised myself that I would never do it again.

But, about a month later, the entire scenario repeated itself. Again, it was late at night and everyone had gone to bed. I concocted some excuse to tell my wife that I had to work on a project for my boss—the first of many lies. This time, however, I locked the door. I knew what I was doing was wrong, and I didn't want to get caught.

Once again, I went online to see what was there. What I found was beyond anything I could've ever imagined. There were pictures of women posing provocatively, and there were images of couples together in very explicit scenes. The content of the pictures ranged from erotic to hardcore. There were seemingly millions of pictures of eighteen- and nineteen-year-old girls. On occasion I would stumble upon something really disgusting, like people having sex with animals. But with the click of the mouse, I could quickly exit that Web site and surf onto something more appealing. It was a pornographic smorgasbord with some really appetizing stuff and some stuff I'd rather pass over. But that is what made the whole experience difficult to resist! I could surf from site to site in search of more tantalizing choices. If I happened upon something unappetizing, I could quickly bypass it. All the time I kept telling myself that at least I wasn't as bad as the guys who chose to look at the illegal and downright bizarre stuff.

In the beginning, I went porn-surfing only once in a while. Before long, however, I found myself looking forward to the times I could be alone on the computer. I found myself returning to some of the same sites. Sometimes I explored different sites. It all depended on how much time I had and my mood at the moment. I found the whole experience very arousing and exciting. I found myself making excuses for my behavior. If my wife wasn't "in the mood" or if I'd a hard day at work, I convinced myself that it was OK to go online. I realize now that these excuses only served to justify what I was doing. I knew it was wrong. But I was still drawn to it. And afterwards I would feel depressed and ashamed. I was too embarrassed to talk to anyone about what I was doing. How could I tell my pastor? How could I tell my best friend? How could I tell my wife? I was too ashamed to reveal my secret sin, but the guilt was overwhelming. I made countless promises to myself not to do it again. Sometimes I was successful, sometimes not. I could go for days and even weeks without looking. And when I slipped up, I prayed for forgiveness and the strength to change. But the temptation seemed too difficult to resist.

As time went on, I learned about chatrooms where people would "trade" pictures. The more I emailed pictures back and forth with people I didn't know, the more I came to believe that what I was doing wasn't all that bad. How could it be when I would chat with other guys online— other *Christian* guys—who also found this stuff nearly impossible to resist. Must be normal, right? Over time I began feeling less guilty and self-conscious about my activity because there were seemingly so many other guys doing the very same thing.

I'd convinced myself that what I was doing wasn't hurting anyone and that it wasn't affecting me or my family. But I was wrong. For starters, it affected my sexual relationship with my wife. Online I would see pictures and video clips of women and couples doing things that I wanted to re-enact with my wife. I found myself wanting sex with her more often and getting frustrated that she wasn't responding the way the women did online. They wanted it all the time and could never get enough. But my wife seemed satisfied with making love once a week. I started thinking that something must be wrong with her. But it was me. My thoughts, my expectations were being warped by what I was seeing online.

My porn use also affected my relationships with my children. While I never fully abandoned them, I do know that I missed out on an awful lot these past three years. Soon they will be off to college and our nest will be empty. And for the rest of my life I will regret what could have been.

Most importantly, my use of Internet porn affected my relationship with God. I can honestly say that over these past three years I saw a gradual decline in the amount of time I spent in prayer and devotions. Before my addiction escalated, I would go to worship and sing God's praises and totally concentrate on the pastor's message. But then things changed. I became more like a hollow shell. I was going through the motions, but never fully engaged. I was turning away from God. By failing to resist the temptation, my time, my energy, and my soul were lured away from my Lord.

And it all started out of simple curiosity.

Curiosity *Can* Kill the Cat

Most Christian men will admit, even if only to themselves, that sexual temptation confronts them on a daily basis. Living in an overly sexualized society, men are constantly bombarded with erotic and explicit images. Whether it's billboard advertising or commercials on TV, the swimsuit edition of *Sports Illustrated* or the *Victoria's Secret* catalogue, men constantly encounter images that capture their visual attention and tempt their souls. What makes these images so difficult to resist is that men are, by God's design, visual creatures. The male body is "wired" to respond emotionally and physically to something attractive.

In early adolescence, boys begin to realize the powerful draw of visual stimulation. Most men can recall sitting in a junior-high classroom, totally captivated by a girl they considered beautiful. It was infatuation, pure and simple, a response to visual stimulation. As young men begin to mature and develop emotionally, the visual attraction becomes coupled with a desire for emotional and relational intimacy resulting in courtships, expressions of love, and covenant vows of marriage. However, at their core, men remain wired to respond to visual stimuli. When exposed to pornography, there is a natural, physiological reaction. A *powerful* reaction. One that is hard to resist.

Many men struggle with the temptation to use the Internet to look at pornography. In a moment of weakness, some will look out of curiosity. They've heard all the rumors about the abundance of titillating images and think they'll "just take a peek" to check it out. Some may do just that and never repeat the indiscretion. Others, however, find themselves returning to the virtual world of cyberporn time and again. The reality is that nearly sixty percent of all visits to Web sites are sexual in nature.[1] According to comScore Media Metrix, 71.9 million people visited adult sites in August 2005, reaching 42.7 percent of the Internet audience.[2]

Those in the porn industry know full and well that their product is tempting and hard to resist. More than that, they are keenly aware of just how addictive pornography can be. In fact, their entire marketing strategy is built upon the reality that a person can become addicted. The approach taken by the porn industry is to distribute their product for free, doing so with the confidence that after a short while the user will become hooked and then begin to pay in order to access the material. By distributing their product for free, the industry manipulates and preys upon curiosity-seekers and those who succumb to temptation. As of July 2007 a websearch using Google with key words "free porn" generated 23 million webpages. Even though they offer much of their product for free, the pornography industry still manages to generate more than $97 billion in worldwide revenues.[3]

Dogs, Pigeons, and Computer Mice

Most of the clients who seek help at the Hope and Recovery Institute describe how their problems with Internet pornography began out of curiosity. They all insist that they never would've considered going into an adult bookstore, but felt safe exploring pornography from the privacy of their own homes. With no one to see them and potentially expose and embarrass them, they felt safe to satisfy their curiosity behind closed doors.

Most clients tell similar stories of lives spiraling out of control. Of course, none of them intended for or even anticipated this consequence. In fact, many of them believed that they *were* in control. They were managing their cyberporn use. They were "just looking." But for each of them something happened that forced them to realize that, because of the porn, their lives were no longer manageable. Whether it was a spouse's discovery of their porn use, a child stumbling upon a surprising secret on the home computer, or disciplinary action by an employer for violating the company's Internet-use policy, something happened which made them realize they had a big problem on their hands.

What had begun as simple curiosity had morphed into something far more sinister and problematic. The changes

Risk Factors

There are three key factors that influence sexual expression and interaction on the Internet. Known as the Triple-A Model (as developed by Dr. Al Cooper, the Clinical Director at the San Jose Marital and Sexuality Center)[4], these conditions make people vulnerable to the powerful temptation to use the Internet to view pornography or engage in other cybersexual behavior:

Accessibility. The cold, stark reality is that pornography and cybersexual material is available twenty-four hours a day, seven days a week. You don't even need to leave the comfort of your home to access it.

these people experienced were the result of a psychological phenomenon known as conditioning.

Anyone who's ever owned a cat or a dog knows the fundamental principle of conditioning, which was studied and documented by Russian scientist Ivar Pavlov. Pavlov conditioned his dogs to salivate whenever they heard a bell ring. He did this simply by ringing a bell any time he fed his dogs. Before long, the dogs began to salivate when they heard sound of the bell because they associated that sound with food. The mere ringing of the bell, even with no food in sight, was enough to get the dogs aroused.

Something similar happens to those who use their computers to access pornography and engage in cybersexual behavior. They begin to associate a computer and the Internet with sexual stimulation. Whether it's the sound of the computer modem, the gentle hum of the computer fan, or clicks on the keyboard, people can become conditioned to associate these auditory stimulations with sexual arousal. Curiosity-seekers are unaware that

Affordability. As mentioned above, there are more than 23 million pornography sites available free of charge. No credit card. No debit card. No contracts. No obligation. It's all free—until a sexual addiction compels the user to take out his American Express or Visa card.

Anonymity. From the privacy of their home or office, persons who surf the Internet for sexual material do so believing they're doing it anonymously. They log on to the Internet using screen names that cloak their identities. People enter virtual reality believing it's a vast masquerade ball.

their minds and bodies are being conditioned to associate the computer with pleasurable feelings of sexual arousal. The result is that their capacity to resist temptation erodes, placing them at risk of developing personal or relational problems, even cyber-sexual addiction.

While Pavlov worked with dogs to demonstrate the principle of conditioning, another scientist worked with birds. B.F. Skinner was a psychologist who developed what came to be known as the "Skinner Box," a device in which he studied the

Warning Signs

The following are warning signs that a person's use of the Internet has progressed from a momentary spiritual lapse (curiosity) to a something far more problematic:

A change in sleep habits. In a desire to not get "caught in the act," those using their computers to access pornography will do so only when they have privacy. In the context of marriage or family, such time can be limited. As a result, those whose curiosity becomes habit-forming will deliberately alter their sleep habits. Some will complain of insomnia. Others will claim a need "to get some work done on the computer" and come to bed later or rise earlier in the morning.

Moodiness and irritability. Although pornography can be physically stimulating, arousing, and pleasurable, most Christians who've fallen to the temptation of pornography are well aware that their behavior is unacceptable. This inner conflict often manifests itself in moodiness and irritability. When struggling with the burden of sexual temptation, those who are typically light-hearted and jovial can appear depressed and often develop a rather short-fused temper.

Demand for privacy. As curiosity becomes a habit, some will move the computer to a more private location, perhaps in a room behavior of pigeons. In a case of truth-is-stranger-than-fiction, much of Skinner's research was underwritten by the American government, which hoped Skinner could train homing pigeons to operate as kamikaze navigators aboard missiles.

To condition his pigeons, Dr. Skinner placed his pigeons in a box equipped with disk upon which the pigeon must peck in order to get a pellet of food. By trial and error, the pigeons quickly learned that pecking on the disk delivered a pellet of food. So well trained were Skinner's pigeons, they were able

with a lock on the door. They may rearrange the furniture so the computer screen is not visible by others in the room. Most often they will become easily irritated when interrupted while on the computer.

Disregarding other responsibilities. Some people can become so absorbed in their online activities that they no longer attend to household chores or other family activities. Time once spent cleaning the kitchen or doing yard work is exchanged for time spent surfing porn sites. Interest in hobbies and other recreational pursuits seems to diminish while time at the computer escalates. Time once invested in attending a child's school or sports activities dissipates, while online pursuits become the focus of considerable attention.

Change in sexual appetite. The sexual stimulation experienced in "virtual reality" causes changes in real-life sexual relationships. For some it manifests itself in an increased libido, or sex drive. For others, it's a change in regard to types of sexual activity desired. Still others withdraw and seem less interested in sexual contact. Having released sexual energy while online, little is left for "real" sex with their marriage partner.

to learn the exact number of pecks required to get the desired pellet. Some pigeons were required to peck five times on the disk, others ten or fifty times. With their little pigeon brains, Skinner's birds learned that if they pecked they would get what they wanted: food.

The funny thing about Skinner's experiment is that toward the end of his work he started running out of pigeon food. This caused great consternation among his subjects. The pigeons' behavior, though, demonstrated the power and drive behind a conditioned behavior. Even without the reinforcement of food pellets, the birds pecked continuously, believing the reward would be imminent.

Poor pigeons.

Poor cyberporn user.

Dr. Tom Grundner, author of the *The Skinner Box Effect*[5], demonstrates that a human being's behavior can become conditioned by Internet pornography. Like pigeons that receive the reinforcement of a food pellet, humans experience a reward of sorts by viewing material that is sexually provocative and arousing. Pornography is pleasing to the eye, and with every click of the mouse that reward is reinforced. With every click of the mouse, a person becomes conditioned to expect more and more. In Grunder's words, computers with Internet access are nothing more than "high-tech Skinner boxes."

There's a big difference, though, between human beings who use a computer mouse to surf for porn and Pavlov's dogs or Skinner's pigeons. Eventually, the dogs got enough to eat and stopped salivating. Eventually, the pigeons got their fill of pellets and stopped pecking. The human appetite, however, is different. When it comes to the rewards of cybersexual stimulation, the human appetite changes over time.

With every click of the mouse, a person believes that the next image will be more stimulating than the one before. It may or may not be, but the individual keeps clicking anyway. In time, the sexual appetite becomes insatiable. The person begins to desire something more—more provocative, more stimulating, more exciting. The process continues until the "perfect" image is found that causes climax through masturbation.

Just as dogs and pigeons have their appetites satisfied when fed, users of Internet pornography believe that their sexual appetites are satisfied after a session of surfing results in orgasm. This, however, is a false perception and why so many persons who access pornography out of curiosity put themselves at risk of greater problems. Although orgasm signals the end of the event, their appetites continue to grow and change.

In the initial stages, when one first explores the world of Internet pornography, it does not take much to achieve stimulation and arousal. Over the course of time, however, individuals discovers that in order to achieve the same level of arousal or experience the same euphoric feeling, they must either spend more time with the material or seek images that are progressively more stimulating. The issue is one of tolerance. Just as someone who is developing a drinking problem begins to notice that it takes more alcohol to experience the same effect as before, so does a user of Internet pornography discover the need for more or "stronger" images. In the early stages, erotic images of scantily clad people are enough to achieve the desired effect. But then the appetite for pornography changes. As it does, the person begins seeking images of people engaged in particular sex acts, or ventures into chatrooms, or desires the novelty of video downloads or live two-way interaction. Others may find their curiosity (now a conditioned response) leading them to explore interaction with increasingly younger persons or to view bizarre or perhaps illegal material.

Those who venture into the virtual world of pornography put themselves at risk, because the psychological phenomenon known as conditioning can actually shape their sexual appetite.

Graham Crackers, Corn Flakes, and Sexual Self-Control

Health food and diet plans are not new phenomena. About 150 years before the South Beach Diet or the low-carb craze, a gentleman by the name of Sylvester Graham pioneered America's first health food crusade. He advocated the consumption of bland foods and the elimination of meat from one's diet. His concern was not for cholesterol or weight management. Graham (the inventor of the graham cracker) believed that spicy foods contributed to erotic thoughts and sexual excesses, which he considered to be masturbation and sexual intercourse more often than once a month.

Another health food advocate, James Caleb Jackson, also linked the ideas of nutrition and sexual self-control. He invented America's first cold cereal made from something similar to crushed graham crackers. He called his product "granola." A few years later, John Harvey Kellogg, nutritionist and campaigner against the "dangers" of masturbation, introduced another health food known as corn flakes. Like Graham's crackers and Jackson's granola, Kellogg's bland concoction was intended to curb one's sexual appetite.

Although crackers and cold cereals have never proven effective at curbing sexual thoughts or behavior, there was a singular goal that led to their invention: the need for sexual self-control.

As suggested by the Apostle Paul, "Do you not know that your body is a temple of the Holy Spirit within you, which you have from God?" (1 Cor. 6:19). Our bodies are to be treated as temples. Our bodies are to be tended as places where God is worshipped and glorified. Anything that is brought into a temple that dishonors God is a desecration.

Graham and Kellogg weren't far from the mark when they campaigned against diets that included too much spice. They simply focused on the wrong appetite. Consumption of pornography literally *does* contribute to sexual excess. And, since it has no redeeming value nor does it in any way reflect the divine, it should be eliminated from the diet.

Scriptural Guidance
for Dealing with Temptation

At that time Jesus came from Nazareth in Galilee and was baptized by John in the Jordan. As Jesus was coming up out of the water, he saw heaven being torn open and the Spirit descending on him like a dove. And a voice came from heaven: "You are my Son, whom I love; with you I am well pleased."

At once the Spirit sent him into the desert, and he was in the desert forty days, being tempted by Satan. He was with the wild animals, and angels attended him.

MARK 1:9–13. NIV

Christians know that evil exists not just because the Bible says so. We know it because we experience it. It's impossible to pick up a newspaper or turn on the news and not recognize that there are powerful destructive forces at work in our world. Those acquainted with the world of Internet pornography and cybersex can offer testimony that the Prince of Darkness is real, alive, and flourishing. They can give testimony because they have suffered from or struggled with pornography. For them, the story of Jesus' wilderness experience provides great hope. This is the story of how Jesus wrestled with Satan in the desert for forty days and emerged victorious from that wilderness experience.

In reading Mark's account of Jesus' baptism and temptation experience, note how quickly the author transitions from one scene to the next. In one sentence God declares his love for Jesus, and in the very next sentence the Spirit "sent" him into the wilderness to be tempted by Satan. In the Revised Standard Version, it translates that the Spirit "drove" Jesus out into the wilderness. In one moment Jesus celebrates his divine calling, while in the very next his mission is put to the test. In one moment a voice from heaven ordains his ministry, and in the very next he is sent into the wilderness to test his resolve to resist temptation and to fulfill his calling to his divine mission.

In the faith community we believe that God has called us to be his followers. We may not literally hear a voice speak from heaven, but we experience it nonetheless in our hearts. We sit in church on Sunday morning, celebrating our calling as Christians. But come Monday morning, we face temptations—temptations that may distract us from our true calling as Christ's disciples.

In the wilderness Jesus was tempted. The other gospel accounts of Jesus' wilderness experience speak of very real temptations like hunger. Jesus was tempted to turn stones into loaves of bread so that he could appease his hunger. There is nothing evil about hunger. Hunger is a natural consequence of being human. Our bodies exert energy, and that energy must be replenished by rest and nourishment. Similarly, there is nothing evil about sexual desire. Sexual desire is also a natural consequence of being human.

So how did Jesus resist the temptation to satisfy his need for hunger? And what would that mean for those who struggle with the temptation to satisfy sexual urges outside of the context of a marriage relationship?

The story of Jesus' wilderness experience shows us how Jesus kept his focus on God. Although faced with very real, powerful temptations, he chose to keep his focus on his baptism experience. He dealt with the temptation to satisfy his own needs by focusing on the reality that God had called him to serve a greater purpose. He dealt with temptation by staying focused on the belief that God would not abandon him.

Just because we Christians are called by God to follow and serve him, we are not exempt from a multiplicity of temptations. Jesus experienced this. But Jesus withstood the agony of temptation by never losing sight of his mission and ministry. For forty days Jesus experienced temptations, and for forty days he discovered the power that helped him keep his focus on the truth—that no matter what Satan would tempt him with, God would be with him. Like Jesus, we can rest assured that even in the wilderness experiences of our lives God will not abandon us.

Regardless of how stimulating or arousing or appealing the temptation may be, God is with us. Regardless of how destructive the dark forces of chaos might be, God does not leave us. Regardless of how much we fear our curiosity may have gotten out of control, God still believes in us.

And just as the text says, God provides angels to minister to us in our wilderness. If we dare to disclose our struggle to fellow believers, God will use them to minister to us. And just as God fortified and strengthened Jesus for his ordeal in the wilderness, so too will we be fortified and strengthened. When the forces of evil inundate us with sexual temptation to the point where we are at risk of being defeated, strength is available to us through God's network of messengers. We just need to muster up the courage to ask for their help.

The faith community recognizes and understands the reality that evil exists. There is evil in the world, and evil attempts to damage our relationship with God. We can be tempted and led astray if we are not watchful and careful. When it comes to pornography, Satan gains a foothold through our curiosity. Of course, curiosity in itself is normal. It is normal to wonder about the world and all that goes on within it. But curiosity can also be the first step to giving into temptation. Some may say, "I was just curious," but normal curiosity can start a process of escalation where they may want to explore "just a little more" or "just a little longer." Before they realize it, their curiosity has become a habit.

In the book of James (a New Testament letter that offers guidance regarding practical aspects of the Christian faith), it is written:

> *"Blessed is the man who perseveres under trial, because when he has stood the test, he will receive the crown of life that God has promised to those who love him. When tempted, no one should say, "God is tempting me." For God cannot bet tempted by evil, nor does he tempt anyone; but each one is tempted when, by his own evil desire, he is dragged away and enticed. Then, after desire has conceived, it gives birth to sin; and sin, when it is full-grown, gives birth to death."*
>
> JAMES 1:12–15, NIV

Evil is a very real presence in our world, and unless Christian men have a specific strategy to resist sexual temptation, they put themselves in jeopardy of being "lured and enticed" by their own desire. Yes, sexual desire is a God-given gift. However, people who use pornography to stimulate that desire risk developing unhealthy sexual desires.

Healthy sexual desire is found in the context of a loving, caring marital relationship. But pornography tempts people to find and explore that desire outside of the covenant relationship of marriage. When people see images of sexually attractive people engaged in intensely provocative activities, their sexual desire is activated or triggered and, if not controlled, can lead to fantasies which contribute to even more unhealthy sexual thoughts. Because their sexual fantasies are no longer focused on their marriage partner, their sexual desire is reduced to nothing more than lust.

It's essential that Christians challenge themselves to control their sexual desires. Failure to do so puts them at risk of embarking on a progression of sexual sin. The initial stage of the cycle is actually pleasurable. When humans first encounter pornography, there is an immediate biological reaction. Within milliseconds of viewing something sensual and provocative, the mind is flooded with sensory messages that convey the message that what is being looked at is good. Spiritually, however, Christians recognize the sinfulness of the material. But the images have a powerful, magnetic force, drawing them to look. Suddenly, the person is confronted with a battle, a battle between biological impulse and spiritual self-control. If in weakness persons use pornography, their spiritual resistance begins to erode, especially if the experience is reinforced by masturbation.

For a Christians who are well aware of the sinfulness of pornography and yet chooses nonetheless to use it, justification of the behavior is the next natural step. They have to rationalize his behavior in order to feel good about themselves, and this only reinforces the cycle. Typically, as the desire for sexual sin increases, the justifications for such behavior also get more elaborate. Justification is a very important factor in the sexual acting-out process. It minimizes the feelings of shame and guilt, which are meant to alert us that our attitudes, perceptions, and behaviors may be morally wrong.

With pornography so readily available on the Internet, Christians are faced with a very real threat to their souls. Like Dave, many Christians will be tempted. Some will resist the powerful grip of pornography, while others will become captive to it.

Strategies for Dealing with Temptation

Take Action Now

Sexual self-control is about more than abstaining from the use of pornography. It is about managing sexual desires and behaviors. Christians should develop an action plan to manage the powerful temptation of pornography. To help you resist the temptation toward cybersexual sin, we recommend you do the following:

Get rid of the computer. While this may not be an option for many people, others may have to ask themselves if they really need to have a computer in their home. In an age where computer terminals are available at most public libraries, you may need to consider living without one.

Change your Internet Service Provider. Many Internet Service Providers, such as America Online® and Comcast®, provide uncensored access to the Internet and World Wide Web. Although these are excellent service providers, the unmonitored access may be too problematic. You may want to consider Internet Service Providers that censor objectionable material.

Install protective software. Many software programs are available that screen and filter pornography. This is strongly recommended, especially for those who have children with access to the computer. Filtering products such as Net-Nanny® and Cybersitter® are good resources, but have limitations (primarily the need to know a porn sites address on the Internet), that prevent them from keeping up with the pace of new porn sites being added to the Internet each day allowing some porn content to get through to your screen. However, a new product called, See No Evil™, is able to prevent objectionable content from reaching your screen because it is not tied to the porn sites address. Instead it blocks content on an image-by-image basis giving a parent total control over the images viewed in their home. See No Evil™ can be downloaded and is available at www.seenoevilonline.com.

Put the computer in a public place. It may not fit with your décor, but having your computer in the living room will discourage the temptation to use the computer to find pornography. It will be more difficult to be secretive this way.

Limit computer time. Covenant with yourself and with your wife to limit the amount of time you spend on the computer. Agree to not use the computer while alone, if possible. Some people find it helpful to set limits on their time. Instead of spending hours on the Internet, try spending one hour a day while other family members are around. If you can't follow this rule, maybe the computer has become a problem.

Delete previously saved material. Many men who have downloaded pornographic images are tempted to keep a collection of material. Keeping this material will only make it easier to relapse and repeat the very behavior you are trying to control. If material has been saved, permanently delete it.

Do something else. If you've found yourself spending time using the computer to access pornography, you need to find something else to do with that time. Whether it's stamp collecting or fly-tying, your thoughts and energy need to be focused elsewhere.

Ask yourself "Why?" Understanding the purpose behind using pornography may actually help you resist the temptation to use it. If you say that you use pornography because you feel lonely, then you may need to focus on developing friendships. If you think pornography helps reduce tension, then you may need to find other ways to manage your stress. If you say that you use porn because something's missing in your marriage, then maybe you need to attempt to resolve the problem rather than compound it.

Not convinced it's a problem? If you're not convinced that pornography is a problem for you and feel that it's mere recreational fun, then we suggest that you give it up for a while. Contract with yourself to refrain from using it for six months. If you aren't able to stay away from pornography for that brief period of time, then maybe you do have a problem after all.

Accountability

Secrecy is Satan's tool. The prince of darkness uses secrecy to undermine our resistance to temptation.

Most Christians use pornography in secret. While they would be too embarrassed to be seen at an adult bookstore, they choose the apparent anonymity of the Internet to access pornography. A driving force that perpetuates this behavior is secrecy. In not wanting their shameful behavior to be exposed, they will go to great lengths to erase the history and delete their computer's temporary Internet files. And all the while they work diligently to avoid being caught, Satan celebrates their gradual spiritual and relational decline. Secrecy gives Satan great satisfaction as Christians grow more and more distant in their relationships with their spouses and their relationships with their God.

A key to resisting temptation, therefore, is revealing the secret. Muster up the courage to admit it. Allow yourself to be held accountable by others in addition to your spouse. Make connections with other Christians who similarly seek to protect themselves. Arrange for regular meetings or contacts with a peer group at your church, or connect with a trusted friend. Knowing that you have to tell someone else about your actions can provide powerful motivation to resist temptation.

Journaling

Another method for successfully resisting temptation is to monitor the factors that might put you at risk. Journaling of daily events is one way to help you develop hypotheses about circumstances that may weaken your resistance. We recommend that you keep a small, pocket-sized notebook with you at all times for approximately four weeks. This is not a "Dear Diary" type of journal but rather a place to record certain events that make you feel sexually tempted. Throughout the day take notice of when you may be dealing with sexual temptation. Note the time, the circumstances immediately before the event, your mood, a description of the event (e.g., content, duration, etc.), and your thoughts afterward. At the end of each day spend a few minutes reviewing your entries. Most likely, you'll notice a pattern. You may discover, for example, that the temptation is greater at certain times of the day. Or it may be influenced more by mood, or factors within your marriage, or circumstances at work. Realizing these patterns will help you learn what requires change.

Some use journaling as a therapeutic tool, writing their sexual autobiography. In fact, many of the vignettes included in this book are excerpts from the autobiographies of clients at The Hope and Recovery Institute. They wrote their stories as part of the therapeutic process to learn more about themselves. In writing their stories, they became better able to reflect on their lives and, in so doing, became more aware of their strengths and coping skills. By writing your sexual history, you too can identify factors that put you at risk of succumbing to sexual temptation.

A WORD FROM DAVE

Fortunately, I have been able to get my behavior back under control. By the grace of God, I made a decision to tell my wife about my struggles. Together we spoke to our pastor, who put me in contact with a small group of men whose stories are similar to mine. Like messengers from heaven, these men have ministered to me in a way I never imagined. They have helped me to be honest with myself. They have helped me to be accountable. They have helped me become a more spiritually mature, more disciplined follower and servant of Jesus Christ.

Can You Handle the Truth?

On Confrontation and Confession

JAN AND STEVE'S STORY

I'm middle-aged, my boobs are beginning to sag, and I have hemorrhoids. To be sure, I wasn't feeling too good about myself. I used to be fairly confident about myself, but my self-esteem began to swirl down the drain when I discovered that my husband was using porn. How was I supposed to compete?

I've known my husband Steve for more than twenty-five years. We were high school sweethearts. We've raised three children, three of whom are now in college. Our youngest son is finishing his senior year in high school. It's always been our dream to make sure all our kids would go to college, and then we'd settle a bit and take some time for ourselves.

Our marriage had been good for the most part. Like most marriages, we've had our ups and down. But I'm not sure there is such a thing as a perfect marriage. We've had our share of financial struggles, but I think we've done well for ourselves. When the kids were younger I was a stay-at-home mom and Steve worked very hard to build his business. Once the kids hit high school, though, I found a job. We needed the money, and with the expense of college tuition for all three of our kids, we knew we'd have to tighten our budget. We weren't wealthy, but we were able to make ends meet. So, life was moving along in a good way. I was happy for the most part, beginning to dream of what life would be like for us as "empty-nesters."

My dreams, though, never involved the problems we were about to encounter. Never in my worst nightmare did I ever imagine that my husband had a problem with pornography.

It was about five years ago when we switched the computer's Internet service provider from a telephone modem to the high-speed cable. I was surprised that Steve was willing to pay the extra expense, but the kids were having to do so much online research for their homework assignments that it seemed reasonable. Not long after, though, we started getting emails advertising porn sites. I asked Steve about it and he told me it was not much to worry about; but I was worried. Worried about my kids. Frankly, I never gave much thought to worrying about Steve.

So, being a good, protective mom, I watched the computer history just to monitor what my kids were up to and one day I did discover that the computer had been used to go to some porn sites. But the record indicated that it happened at a time when the girls were at a church retreat and our son was at a basketball game. I was hurt and angry. I didn't know how to confront him. I guess I was afraid I would find out that after all these years he found me less attractive than he used to. It took me a good week to muster up the courage to talk with Steve and when I did the conversation lasted no more than five minutes. He actually apologized for not telling me that he "accidentally" went into a Web site, not knowing that it was a porn site. He said he tried to click out of it as soon as he realized what it was. He assured me that he didn't tell me because he was concerned that I would be upset.

And I was upset. Not then. But over the next five years we have had this same conversation no less than half a dozen times. And each time he would become more and more angry with me, accusing me of being paranoid and overly suspicious. And each time I would confront him I would come away from the conversation wondering if I was the one with the problem.

But a few months ago I crawled off to bed early. It was a Friday night and I'd had an exhausting week. A few hours later I awoke to discover that Steve had not yet come to bed. I glanced at the clock. It was one o'clock. Steve usually is in bed by eleven. I figured he had fallen asleep on the couch. He's done that before and wakes up with back pain—and in a bad mood. So, to save myself the grief of living with a grump, I went downstairs to get him to come to bed.

I was shocked at what I discovered: Steve sitting at the computer looking at pornography. I gasped. He was startled and quickly turned off the computer monitor. No words were exchanged between us. I went back upstairs, took his pillows and tossed them on the floor outside our bedroom door. He could sleep on the floor for all I cared.

I didn't sleep a wink. I don't think I've ever been that upset.

The next morning I got up not certain what was going to be said or done. I made some coffee. I didn't know what else to do. When Steve came into the kitchen, I asked him if he wanted some coffee. It just seemed like the right thing to do. We sat at the kitchen table for the longest time in silence. I saw the pain in his face, and I'm sure he saw the pain in mine. I finally found the courage to speak. (Maybe God had given me the right words at this time, because I couldn't do all this by myself.) I told Steve I wanted to know everything. The truth. The whole story.

Steve told me that in these past five years he'd been battling with a desire to use pornography and losing. After all these years, after all the times I had confronted him, he finally confessed that what I had suspected was actually true. It was a surreal moment for me. Although blazing with anger that he had lied to me on those many occasions, I was relieved (for lack of a better word) to finally get the truth.

Steve told me that for him, porn was like a drug. Over time he wanted to do it more and more. The more he looked, the more he wanted. It started out of curiosity, he said, but within weeks he looked at it whenever he was at home alone. It didn't take long though, and he would do it when I was in the shower and the kids were downstairs watching TV. He admitted that sometimes he would masturbate while looking at pictures. This was very difficult for me to listen too, but I knew by the shamed look on his face, it also took a lot of courage to disclose this.

As he talked I kept trying to tell myself that this was his problem, not mine. But to be honest I really felt that this was about me. I know I don't look the same as I did when we were first married. I felt sad that maybe he didn't feel attracted to me anymore. And I felt angry that I had to compete with the women in the porn pictures he was looking at. Steve tried to tell me that this wasn't about me, but that is exactly how I felt.

I told him that I had a thousand questions I wanted to ask. I told him I expected to hear the truth. He told me that he would be honest, but asked if we could do something first before I started asking him questions.

He asked if we could pray.

It had been years since we had done that. And in that moment I knew things were going to be alright. We prayed to God asking for guidance to sort through this. We prayed to God asking for strength to keep our marriage together. We prayed to God to help us understand what went wrong.

It has taken a lot of time to sort out all the feelings and confusion. I'm still really angry about pornography. It has touched my family in a deadly way. Sometimes, I still have feelings of rejection and hurt, and when he is home alone, the thought crosses my mind about whether he is looking at pornography again. I think this is all very normal. It takes time to rebuild trust once trust has been shaken. But I have confidence that Steve will win this battle, and I will do my best to be supportive. He knows he has hurt me, but he's trying hard to make up for this. As I told him, the best gift he could give me, was to simply leave pornography alone, once and for all, and make a recommitment to live a Christ-oriented life.

Do You Want the Truth?

Do you want to know the truth? Can you handle the truth? Do you want to know the truth about your partner, yourself, and your marriage? Do you have the courage to confront the truth? Is your partner willing to confess the truth? That is, of course, the purpose of confrontation: to expose the truth so something can be done to right the wrong.

Christian couples face the same kinds of challenges as non-believers. Our faith orientation does not make us immune to temptation or shield us from problems associated with lust. But even though Christians are well-informed about the pro-liferation of pornography on the Internet, many are reluctant to face the truth that their own lives, their own marriages are at risk. Most wives in the Christian community find it difficult to imagine that their husbands could be surfing the Internet for pornography. They consider their husbands (for the most part) to be loving, loyal, kind and considerate. But users of pornography? It just doesn't seem to fit with the type of man they consider their husbands to be. Many wives who later dis-covered their husbands struggled with pornography will tell you that although they suspected that *something* was wrong they never imagined that cyberporn was the culprit. They just could not fathom the idea that the husbands with whom they worship with on Sunday could surf porn sites come Monday morning. Although fully aware that cyberporn is a major prob-lem in the society, many Christian wives can't imagine this is the case with their husbands. But they do sense that some-thing is awry. They don't know what it is exactly, but intuitively they sense that something just isn't right. They have no major marital problems or issues, but they just sense an emotional distancing in the relationship.

Many Christian husbands consider their cybersexual behavior to have little effect on their lives, including their marriage. It may sound crass, but some view their experiences with cyberporn merely to be recreational. Just for fun. Of course, their religious and spiritual foundation makes them fully aware that the behavior reflects a measure of spiritual weakness, but pornography is difficult to resist. The issue, however, is more than temptation. The problem is with perception. Although a visual creature by design, the male mind often fails to see how problematic or damaging pornography can be.

What starts as mere curiosity can quickly escalate to become a cancer-like force that has the power to erode a loving, covenant relationship. A couple is at greatest risk when they fail to heed the warning signs of a potential problem. Wives need to realize that their husbands, by their very nature, are visual creatures and as such are at risk for the sexual temptation available on the Internet. Husbands need to correct their perception and see that their "recreational" use of pornography is causing changes within themselves and causing potentially irreparable damage to the relationship.

A Tip For Concerned Wives: Anticipate Denial

If you suspect that your husband may be struggling with Internet pornography, you (as your husband's spiritual partner) must be courageous enough to confront him. The word "confrontation" itself has negative connotations, suggesting bitterness, anger, and resentment. But confrontation, from a Christian perspective, is an act of accountability that embraces your husband in love for the purpose of encouraging him to be the man God intended for him to become.

When confronted with the reality that life has been polluted by cyberporn, a natural reaction is that of denial. It is important, however, to keep in mind that denial is not just a make-believe, Pollyannaish attempt to pretend that an event is not happening. In the field of psychology, denial is considered a "defense mechanism," and as such it serves a purpose. In the case of confronting cybersexual behavior, the most obvious purpose is self-protection. When confronted with the truth about themselves, men experience a range of emotions including embarrassment, guilt, and fear. Most users of cyberporn believe that their activity on the Internet has been anonymous and not much consideration is given to the possibility of discovery. When confronted, however, the individual experiences a wave of embarrassment and guilt. And just as a swimmer in the ocean braces himself when confronted with a powerful wave of water, so may your husband brace himself with an initial response of denial. In many ways this is normal and to be anticipated. It allows him time (whether a few seconds, hours, or a few days) to sort through his thoughts and come to recognize the reality of what he has been doing.

The best manner to manage denial is to challenge it with information. You need to be able to communicate your concerns and observations. Talk to him about what you have noticed, for example, in regard to irritability or that he has been coming to bed later than usual. You are not being accusatory. You are communicating an observation and wondering if anything is going on. Of course, you must leave open the possibility that he may minimize these things or provide alternative explanations. If you suspect, however, that the problem is associated with pornography, you need to be prepared to present evidence to help him move beyond the denial.

In preparing for a healthy, productive confrontation, the first task is for you to become computer literate. Although we live in a culture in which everything seems to be computer dependent, it is not unusual for many people to possess limited knowledge on how computers operate. If you suspect that someone is struggling with a cybersexual problem, it will be very important for you to develop your knowledge of computers.

We suggest that you learn some basics in regard to checking the Internet history, Web site "cookies," and temporary Internet files. It is important, however, that you first consider your motivations for doing so. The intent is not to find the facts so as to prove your husband's guilt. On the contrary, the intention is to gather information so that you can lovingly challenge the denial to help him move beyond shame and guilt to becoming motivated toward change and renewal. Before you proceed, therefore, we strongly encourage you to pray asking for God to keep your intention focused on problem-solving rather than fault-finding.

If you have a computer that operates on a Windows Operating System, there are two easy methods for checking the computer history:

- Access the Internet Service Provider (for example, click on the icon for AOL, Comcast, or Internet Explorer). On the tool bar, click the History button. The History bar appears, containing links for Web sites and pages visited in previous days and weeks. In the History bar, click a week or day, click a Web site folder to display individual pages, and then click the page icon to display the Web page. To sort or search the History bar, click the arrow next to the View button at the top of the History bar.

- Click on the Start button and scroll up until you find the Control Panel. You can also access this area by clicking on the "My Computer" icon on the computer screen. Click on the Control Panel icon, and a dialogue box will open, offering you access to "Temporary Internet Files." Notice that there are buttons that also delete these files as well as Internet Cookies. Click on "View Files" and a list will appear. These are files that attach to your computer whenever you visit a webpage on the Internet. By scrolling down the list you will be able to discern if any of these sites are pornographic. Be prepared, however, because some of the language associated with these file names is rather graphic and vulgar. Notice also that the information available also indicates the date and time the material was accessed. You may also discover that the information in these files has been deleted. This may cause you concern or alarm if you think it represents a deliberate attempt to hide the computer's history. Be aware, however, that these files do take up disk space and may have been deleted deliberately not for the purpose of "covering tracks" but to open up space on the computer's hard drive.

If you have an Apple/Macintosh System you can check the history in this way:

- First, open your Safari browser by clicking on the Safari icon in the dock. Click on History in your Safari menu, located at the top of your screen. When the drop-down menu appears your most recent history (the last 10 web pages that you have visited) will appear.

- Directly below it you will find the rest of your recorded browsing history, grouped by day into sub-menus. If you have visited more than 10 web pages on the current day, there will also be a sub-menu present labeled Earlier Today containing the rest of today's history.

Even if your husband denies responsibility for the information you discovered on the computer, you have still accomplished a great deal in helping him with a potential problem. Even if he has chosen to not admit a potential problem, you have communicated to him that you have the know-how to check the computer's history. This will contribute to any hesitancy that he may have in the future to access Internet pornography. There is the possibility, however, that he may become more diligent to erase the history in an attempt to "cover his tracks." We would recommend, therefore, that in your initial conversation you covenant with him that no one, except you or another accountability partner, will delete this computer information. Even if he reports to you that porn is not a problem for him, this is a simple way for your husband to demonstrate to you that he has not succumbed to temptation.

Another Tip For Concerned Wives: Consider Motivations

Having gathered information that your husband uses the computer to access pornography or engage in some other form of cybersexual behavior, it is helpful to take time to consider his motivations for doing so. While the impulse may be to immediately confront the problem, we strongly encourage you to prayerfully consider why he may be doing it. Poor preparation

A Note About Monitoring Software

Out of concern that there is a problem, some wives purchase computer software that records the activity conducted on a computer. In some cases this software is loaded onto the computer in "stealth" mode. This means that people using the computer may not be aware that their activity is being monitored. We would discourage the use of such products, at least during the initial stages of confrontation. Clinical experience indicates that wives who chose such an approach often find the confrontation sidetracked away and a premature confrontation may result in even more emotional distance between you and your husband.

Is it merely recreational? It sounds offensive, but the reality is that many men use their computers to access pornography as a form of recreation. For them the sexual act is entirely mechanical. For men, there is no emotional attachment to the persons depicted in the images and the experience is completely devoid of relational intimacy.

Women, however, find it difficult to understand the disconnect between sexual intimacy and emotional intimacy. If your husband's use of porn "means nothing" to him, then communicate to him what it "means" for you. As partners in a covenant relationship, you are bound to honor one another and if pornography jeopardizes this, then it must be jettisoned from the relationship.

Is it a problem in the marriage? Some men say they turn to the computer for pornography because they feel a sense of sexual neglect from their wives. Hearing this, many women become angry, feeling as if their husbands are projecting blame onto to them. For many couples, therefore, the

from the original intention. Although the software provides data that is used as "evidence," the typical response is complaints of a breach of privacy. Unfortunately, the conversation becomes convoluted as the wife defends her own trustworthiness. It is recommended instead that you gather information in regard to history, cookies, and temporary Internet files. As described above, keep the conversation focused on the problem and on how to develop a strategy toward positive change.

process of confrontation is quickly derailed as they attempt to affix blame on each other.

In order to keep the process of confrontation and confession productive, couples need to recognize that the use of pornography may represent and reflect a failure of marital communication. Not the wife's failure. Not the husband's failure. But a failure of marital communication. Use of pornography may be symptomatic of a problem within the marriage relationship. For some couples, there are unspoken sexual issues that date back to the early days of their marriage, but the couple has learned to avoid addressing them. Solving the problem, therefore, requires a willingness to address the issues.

Christian marriage, albeit a covenant partnership, is fundamentally a selfish enterprise. That is to say that two people are in relationship because the need each other. Two people are in relationship because they have needs that must be satisfied. For a multiplicity of reasons, you need your spouse to be in your life. Your spouse also needs you. When each of you feel as if your needs are met, then you feel good about yourselves and each other. However, the moment one of you feels that your needs are being neglected, there is a break in the harmonious relationship. Mutual needs are no longer being satisfied and the relationship is put at risk. In healthy relationships, couples are able to communicate their sense of dissatisfaction and negotiate changes so that both persons can feel satisfied. In a healthy relationship it is a collaborative effort at satisfying each other's needs.

When it comes to sex, a healthy Christian marriage needs to be mutually satisfying. But many couples find it difficult to talk about sex. Even when a Christian couple has joined together in the intimacy of sex, they nonetheless feel awkward talking about the subject. As such, many couples fail to address issues of frequency, initiation, and the various types of sexual activities that married couples can enjoy. The failure to communicate may lead to resentment. The consequential sense of neglect may contribute to a decision to use pornography.

It must be understood, however, that this does not affix blame on the wife. It is the husband who has chosen to use pornography and he must understand that from his wife's perception this is a violation of the covenant relationship. But for couples for which his behavior is associated with a disturbance in the sexual relationship, the key for remedy is the development of communication skills and reaching collaborative agreement so that both can feel sexually satisfied.

Could it be something else? Prior to any confrontation it is essential that consideration be given to other explanations for the behavior. This is not to minimize the problem, but to suggest that the behavior may be a reflection of some other psychological phenomenon. It is strongly encouraged, therefore, that persons struggling with issues related to pornography consult with a mental health professional to determine if the use of pornography is symptomatic of a more extensive problem.

Some people who suffer from depression look for ways to self-medicate. More than feeling "blue," depressed people agonize with painful emotions. Some turn to alcohol, others to drugs, as they seek to find ways to soothe the pain. Some discover their "medication" in Internet pornography. Why? Because it is visual material which elicits a physiological response. Any human being who has ever been sexual recognizes that sexual activity creates pleasurable physiological changes. There is no need to drink alcohol or ingest drugs. The human body can create its own chemical change by becoming sexually aroused and stimulated. For persons who are experiencing a mood disorder, this causes a temporary alleviation of the depression. The fix, however, is temporary, and similar to alcohol and drugs, actually compounds the depression. Although the chemical "high" during the sexual experience seems to provide relief, the sense of shame and regret afterwards contributes to an even more profound depression. Some persons, seeking relief again from the agony of depression, repeat the cycle time and time again, continuing the downward spiral of depression.

There are others who experience what is called a "bi-polar" depression. For these individuals, their mood disorder is punctuated not only with periods of depression but also moments of heightened energy. In the field of mental health, these periods are referred to as "manic" or "hypomanic" episodes. During these times, bipolar persons become uncharacteristically more talkative while others attend to chores or other activities like the Energizer® rabbit. For some, this energy is expressed sexually. More than an active libido, the person's sex drive is kicked into overdrive. Their partners feel as if they "can't keep up." Unlike a person with a normal "high" sex-drive, persons experiencing a hypomanic/manic episode sense that they can't get enough or feel as if their sexual appetite is insatiable. For a bipolar person, therefore, heightened sexual activity (including excessive pursuit of pornography) is reflective of a hypomanic or manic episode.

Obsessive Compulsive Disorder is one of the most common mental disorders. Research indicates that 6.5 million people struggle with OCD, which is an anxiety disorder that involves recurrent obsessions or compulsions.[1] Obsessions are intrusive thoughts, impulses, or images. Some people suffering from OCD have recurrent worrisome thoughts that they may have forgot to turn off the coffee pot or forgotten to lock the door. Throughout the day their thoughts are focused and concentrated on the overwhelming worry that their home may burn-down or be burglarized. Compulsions are behaviors that a person feels compelled to perform in order to diffuse the compulsive thoughts such as returning home to check the coffee pot or to verify that the door has been locked. While on the surface this may seem anything but problematic (and perhaps practical), but a person with OCD would return home on multiple occasions, experiencing the same anxious thoughts time after time. For some people, the obsessions involve thoughts or sex. Without cue or provocation the individual experiences intrusive thoughts about sex and sexual interaction and it is as if the thoughts become trapped in their minds. They obsess on these thoughts and find relief only by acting on the impulse. Because research indicates that 6.5 million people suffer from OCD (being one of the most common mental disorders), some experts believe that cybersexual behavior is a symptom of this disorder.

Scriptural Guidance
for Confrontation and Confession

One evening David got up from his bed and walked around on the roof of the palace. From the roof he saw a woman bathing. The woman was very beautiful, and David sent someone to find out about her. The man said, "Isn't this Bathsheba, the daughter of Eliam and the wife of Uriah, the Hittite? Then David sent messengers to get her. She came to him, and he slept with her. (She had purified herself from her uncleanness.) Then she went back home. The woman conceived and sent word to David, saying, 'I am pregnant.'

In the morning David wrote a letter to Joab and sent it with Uriah. In it he wrote, "Put Uriah in the front line where the fighting is fiercest. Then withdraw from him so he will be struck down and die.

So while Joab had the city under siege, he put Uriah at a place where he knew the strongest defenders were. When the men of the city came out and fought against

Joab, some of the men in David's army fell; moreover, Uriah the Hittite was dead.

When Uriah's wife heard that her husband was dead, she mourned for him. After the time of mourning was over, David had her brought to his house, and she became his wife and bore him a son. But the thing David had done displeased the Lord.

The Lord sent Nathan to David. When he came to him, he said, "There were two men in a certain town, one rich and the other poor. The rich man had a very large number of sheep and cattle, but the poor man had nothing except one little ewe lamb he had bought. He raised it, and it grew up with him and his children. It shared his food, drank from his cup and even slept in his arms. It was like a daughter to him.

Now a traveler came to the rich man, but the rich man refrained from taking one of his own sheep or cattle to prepare a meal for the traveler who had come to him. Instead, he took the ewe lamb that belonged to the poor man and prepared it for the one who had come to him.

David burned with anger against the man and said to Nathan, "As surely as the Lord lives, the man who did this deserves to die! He must pay for that lamb four times over, because he did such a thing and had no pity."

Then Nathan said to David, "You are the man."

2 SAMUEL 11:2–5; 14–15; 16–17; 12:1–7A, NIV

Sooner or later, men who regularly use pornography are confronted with the realization that their cybersexual behavior is out of control. And when confronted, they have a choice: denial and rationalization or facing the truth.

Even though they are well aware of what they are doing, men often convince themselves that their activities have been done in complete secrecy and anonymity. They have been able to protect their secret from exposure, believing that what they do behind closed doors is unknown and undetectable. And when confronted, men are forced to shift their thinking. Confrontation means that either they maintain the charade of secrecy or they recognize that their sin has been exposed and jig is up.

Those who have ever had a problem with pornography are familiar with rationalization. For them, there is a phrase that echoes in their thoughts over and over again which begins with the words, "At least I'm not."

"At least I'm not having a real affair." "At least I'm not looking at kiddie porn." "At least I'm not pressuring my wife to do the things she doesn't want to do." "At least I'm not paying for it; I'm only looking at free stuff." "At least I'm not doing it when my kids are around." "At least I'm not into really kinky and perverted stuff." "At least I'm not a letch around other women." "At least I'm not at the strip clubs or adult bookstores." "At least I'm not meaning it when I cyber with those people."

Men often go astray and enter the valley of the shadow of self-deception. That is what happened with David. David was in the valley of the shadow of self-deception when God sent the prophet Nathan to get him turned around. Nathan told David about a poor man who had only one sheep that he had raised as a family pet. The poor man's children had played with the sheep, and the animal had been fed from their table. One day, their neighbor, a rich man with large flocks, took the poor man's one sheep and killed it, serving it to a visitor.

As a former shepherd, King David was indignant. He was incensed. He demanded to know the rich man's name so that he could be punished. Nathan said simply, "That man is you."

It was the moment of truth.

In that instant an unimaginable surge of shame must have welled up within David. A lump in his throat. A knot in his stomach. Faced with the truth, this was a moment for decision.

No doubt about it, he had a choice. Nathan had no authority over him. David was the King. He knew he could dance around Nathan's accusation. He had the power and the authority and finesse to dodge the bullet of truth. But in that moment David made a decision to become radically committed to moral purity. In that moment of truth, David was able to face his shame, the shame of realizing what he had done. Had he only taken a sheep from Uriah, David could have restored it a hundredfold. But he could not give back a life that he had destroyed. He could not give back a life he had taken away. He could not undo the past. There was no rewind button.

Sooner or later the truth about what we are doing is exposed. Maybe it will be when you get a call from Human Resources and they inform you that you have been fired for violating the company's Internet-use policy. Maybe it will be when your child stumbles upon something you downloaded but forgot to delete. Maybe it will be when you find yourself arranging for a real-life meeting with someone you have been cybering with. Maybe it will be when the knock at the door is not UPS delivery, but an agent from the FBI. Or maybe it will be when your partner asks, "Honey, how is it with you? Has it been a problem?" Maybe it will be when you read the story of David and when you get to Nathan's line, "You are the man," and you realize that God is talking to you.

What do you do when confronted with the truth? You have a choice. You can continue to live a life of deceit, deceiving yourself, deceiving your partner. Or you can do what David and Bathsheba did. You face the consequences. What happened to David and Bathsheba? Their first child died. It is inconceivable that God would cause the death of an infant because of his father's sin, and so it is not suggested that others who are guilty of sexual sin would be punished in such a way. But there will be consequences. And as it says in Scripture, the wages of sin is death.

When it comes to persons or couples struggling with cybersexual problems, something has to die. Old patterns of denial, patterns of self-deception, patterns of rationalization, all have to die. Are you afraid that maybe your marriage won't be able to survive if you disclose your struggle? There is no guarantee it will, but as a Christians you have been given faith to trust in the power of resurrection. And before there is resurrection there must be death. For you, this might mean that certain aspects of that old relationship, old expectations, and old ways of relating have to die.

When faced with the truth, when faced with his shame, David accepted the consequences. And when he heard about the child's death, he got up, took a bath, covered his body with lotions, put on clean clothes, and went to pray in the house of the Lord. He came back again and ate, and then went in to comfort Bathsheba. Do not miss the powerful symbolism of what he did when he made a decision to be radically committed to moral purity. By accepting the truth about himself, there was no need to continue living a life of self-deception. He was washed clean. He was forgiven. He turned to a place of worship to give honor to God who made it possible. He nourished himself spiritually and physically and he pledged his love and support to Bathsheba.

Years later David wrote a psalm that has special meaning for those who have walked in the shadows of shame and self-deception:

> *The Lord is my shepherd,*
> *I shall not be in want.*
> *He makes me lie down in green pastures,*
> *He leads me besides quiet waters,*
> *He restores my soul.*
> *He guides me in the paths of righteousness*
> *For his names sake.*

Even though I walk
Through the valley of the shadow of death,
I will fear no evil,
For you are with me;
Your rod and your staff,
They comfort me.
You prepare a table before me
In the presence of my enemies.
You anoint my head with oil;
My cup overflows.
Surely goodness and love will follow me
All the days of my life,
And I will dwell in the house of the Lord Forever.

PSALM 23, NIV

As Christians we believe in the power of resurrection. We believe there is hope not only for the sinner, but also for those who have been sinned against. By the power of resurrection there is a second chance not only for those who go on living, but also for those whose lives have been destroyed by sin. We believe that the resurrection means that someday the tangled web we have created will be straightened out. Righteousness will be restored, and we will dwell in the house of the Lord forever.

Strategies for Confrontation and Confession

The purpose of any confrontation is to discern and determine the truth. The truth, however, can be difficult to face. Prayer, therefore, is an opportunity for you to seek guidance from God as you prepare to encounter the truth. Prayer will help you develop the appropriate tone for the conversation. Prayer will allow you to confront with supportive understanding and confess with resolute honesty. Prayer will help you prepare for what you may learn and discover in the process of confrontation. You are, after all, afraid of what you may find. You are concerned about your spouse's reaction. You may fear your own reaction. You may struggle with embarrassment over having to talk about sex and sexuality. Prayer will be an opportunity to contemplate these things and present them to God seeking guidance and wisdom.

For those who find it difficult to find words to express, the following prayers are suggested:

A Wife's Prayer

Gracious God, you know how nervous I am. I know something is bothering my husband, and there is part of me that is not wanting to face what it may be. But I think I know what it is, but I am just so afraid. Afraid of what I might discover about him; afraid of what this might mean about me. I'm just so afraid.

But I do trust you, O God, and so I pray for your blessing upon us in this difficult time. You blessed us on our wedding day when we made our covenant pledge to one another, promising to love each other for better, for worse, in sickness and in health. But this is not the kind of sick I anticipated, O God. I am sick in the heart and wounded in spirit. But you, O God, have blessed us throughout our marriage and I trust in your continued blessings as we try to work through this. You are our God and you brought us together and you have blessed us with a good history and I pray that our history will be a strong foundation to help us withstand this current storm.

I need your help, Lord. Help our marriage to be strong enough so that we can talk about this without anger and hostility. Help me to communicate my feelings to him while at the same time being understanding of his struggle. Help me to listen in a supportive way. Help me to choose my words carefully so that I am not judgmental, but encourage him to be the man you intend him to be.

The presence of your Spirit was apparent in the life of King David when he was confronted by the prophet Nathan. And so I pray, Lord, let your Spirit be upon us. May your Spirit grant us compassion, strength, and a resolution to make our marriage stronger than it was before. And give us both the strength to resist the temptations, which have drawn us away from each other and away from you. Amen.

A Husband's Prayer

Who have I been trying to fool, O Lord? You know my thoughts. You know what I have done. And you know my shame. I have been dishonest with myself and with my wife. And I certainly have failed to live the Christian life to which you have called me.

I do not understand why pornography has such power over me and why I find it difficult to resist the temptation to look. But I do know that you give strength to those who ask and through all my struggles I have been less than sincere in requesting your help. But now, O Lord, I need you to strengthen me. Not strength to resist, but the strength and courage to be honest with my wife. I am so afraid of how she will react. This is my problem, not hers, and I do not want to burden her or cause her pain. But it's as if I've been living a double-life, and in an awful way I feel I have betrayed her trust by keeping this a secret from her. Bless her, Lord. And by your Spirit, may I have the courage to be the man you intend me to be. Amen.

Setting the Stage

When people commit themselves to the process of confrontation and confession, much time and energy should be invested into preparation of what will be said. Obviously, this preparation is invaluable, as it will set the tone for healing to begin. Couples need to be cautious, however, in recognizing that "speaking" is only a fraction of the communication process. Of course you prepare yourself for what you want to say. But have you adequately prepared yourself to listen?

If you are praying for God's Spirit to guide you through a productive exchange of confrontation and confession, you may find inspiration in reading the story of Pentecost in the Book of Acts. When the Holy Spirit came upon those gathered in Jerusalem, a miracle happened:

> *Suddenly a sound like a violent wind came from heaven and filled the whole house where they were sitting. They saw what seemed to be tongues of fire that separated and came to rest on each of them. All of them were filled with the Holy Spirit and began to speak in other tongues as the Spirit enabled them."*
>
> *"Now there were staying in Jerusalem God-fearing Jews from every nation under heaven. When they heard this sound, a crowd came together in bewilderment, because each one heard them speaking in his own language.*

ACTS 2:2–6

Of the countless blessings experienced that day, not the least of which was the gift of hearing. Though different languages were being spoken, the power of the Holy Spirit enabled them to hear and understand what was being said. And so, as you prayerfully prepare for confrontation and confession, you need to do more than anticipate your own words or tone. You need to focus attention on how well you will listen to each other.

Wives: Consider Tone, Timing, and Terrain

Pay attention to the manner in which the prophet Nathan approached King David. He was well aware of David's transgressions, but in confronting him, he elected to use a metaphor designed to provoke a sympathetic response. Once a shepherd boy himself, David was indignant at the story of a man who slaughtered a family pet. The prophet's wisdom was to put the conversation in an emotional context. The prophet approached an emotionally charged and potentially volatile subject in such a manner so that David would be emotionally prepared to recognize his sin.

In confronting your husband, you are encouraged to approach him in a manner that elicits more honesty and less defensiveness. Of course you do not have control over his response, but you can work carefully to set the stage for a productive conversation. The first consideration is **Tone**. It may seem silly, but practice out loud what you intend to say. In practicing you will discover that even though you are avoiding language that is harsh and judgmental, you may still be inadvertently communicating judgment through your tone. You may want to consult with a friend who can provide helpful feedback or you may want to use a tape-recorder. By practicing, you are working toward developing a tone that resonates concern and a determination to get the truth.

A second consideration is **Timing**. *When* have you and your husband best communicated? Has it been in the morning at breakfast or in the evening after the kids are in bed? Has it been on a weekday or a weekend? Most people, when reflecting upon their relational history recognize a pattern to their communication style. There are, literally, times that are more conducive for communication than others.

Terrain is another factor to consider. *Where* have you and your husband best communicated? Again, most couples can review their history and recognize that they communicate better in some places as opposed to others. If you have a history of arguing in the bedroom, then you will want to avoid being in that room when confronting him. Whether it is in the kitchen, on the deck, or in the car, find the best place to talk.

Practical Communication Skills

It is estimated that the average rate of speech is spoken at 125 words per minute. The average person, though, can think four times faster, at 500 words per minute. This means that a person's brain can begin formulating a response even as it is receiving verbal information. In many cases this would mean that people are listening with only about twenty-five percent efficiency, actually hearing only one out of every four words. And when the conversation is complicated by heightened emotion (anger, hurt, or frustration), there is a substantial decrease in listening comprehension.

For many couples, communication skills are similar to driving skills. When an individual first learns to drive, there is intense focus and concentration on a multiplicity of factors involved with operating a potential death-machine. Attention is given to speed, traffic patterns, blind spots, and lane changes. After the driver has developed some experience, the focus and the attention begin to slip away. Driving becomes routine, and some experience occasions when they drive their vehicle from point A to point B and upon arrival realize that their thoughts were so pre-occupied with something else they marvel at how they ever made the journey. Something similar occurs with relationships. Early on, couples focus intense attention to communication patterns, carefully crafting the spoken word and attentively listening to what is being said. Over the course of time, though, the couple becomes more comfortable and listening skills slip into autopilot.

Actually hearing only one out of four words, the listening partner's brain (in auto-pilot mode) filters through what they "think" is being communicated. Capturing only ever few words, the listener quickly discerns whether what is being said is important or interesting. The listener's level of engagement in the conversation is reduced to radar, scanning the other's comments for "hot-button" words that the brain has identified as exceptionally meaningful. Just as the phrase "free food" might instantly capture the attention of hungry teenage boys, there are certain vocabulary words in marriage relationships to which the brain is exceptionally sensitive. When it comes to conversations regarding the use of pornography and cybersex, there are words that are typically part of what is being said. Words such as "hate," "disgust," "sickening," "gross," and "angry" are in-and-of-themselves normal and expected components of a conversation focused on something as volatile as pornography. But when the listener is only capturing one out of four words and filtering only the potentially threatening words, there is the potential that the conversation will be disastrous.

There are key skills which, when utilized, help couples become more productive in their ability to communicate. Developing these skills will help couples become more effective and productive when confronting problems associated with cybersexual behavior. These skills include the following:

Body Language: Face your partner squarely. Close proximity is best, conveying the message that this is a relationship problem and that you are willing to confront this "together." Also, be cautious what you do with your posture. Don't cross your arms. You want to convey a willingness to receive a response and you want to avoid the non-verbal communication of judgment. In addition, maintain good eye contact. You are not only looking at your partner's face, you are looking into his heart and indeed his very soul.

Paraphrase: A paraphrase is a process in which you restate in your own words the content of what you have heard the other person. It is not mimicking or parroting verbatim. It is mirroring and rephrasing the other's words so that you know you fully understand what has been spoken. Paraphrasing is an essential skill in that it gives you an opportunity to determine if you have accurately heard what your partner has attempted to communicate. It is also gives your partner a chance to correct you if you have misinterpreted his comments or he can correct himself and rephrase what he intended to communicate.

Paraphrasing is a very time intensive task and many couples fail to invest enough energy in clarifying what is being said and heard. Unfortunately, most marital communication breaks down at the onset of a conversation either because of a failure to paraphrase or an inaccurate interpretation of what has been communicated.

An example of a derailed conversation might sound like this:

> *Wife:* "I'm concerned about how much time you have been spending on the computer lately. With so many men struggling with pornography I wonder how it's been with you."

> *Husband:* "So you think I'm a pervert?"

From the get-go this conversation has been derailed. The husband failed to paraphrase and has become angry (and possibly defensive). In order to prevent this conversation from escalating into an argument, it would be imperative for the wife to rephrase her initial comment and for her to ask her husband to paraphrase. By deliberately slowing the pace of the conversation and working cautiously to be certain that communication is accurately presented and received, there is a greater likelihood of a productive outcome. In this case, the husband could paraphrase "I hear that you're concerned about how much time I've been spending on the computer. And you worry that I might be looking at pornography. Am I right?"

Both the husband and wife have a responsibility to clarify what has been communicated in regard to both nonverbal and verbal communication. In the example above, the husband may comment, "The tone of your voice seems a little judgmental, and I can't help but feel a little defensive."

In regard to paraphrasing, couples must understand that this skill is utilized throughout any conversation wherein clear communication is essential. It is not isolated to only the first few comments, but continues throughout the conversation even to the point of resolution.

Perception Check: A perception check is a communication skill in which you seek clarification on what you think you "see" happening. In a sense you are guessing what is going on, because you truly do not know. All you know is what you see and what you see may not be interpreted accurately. For example, in your conversation with your husband in which you are confronting his use of pornography, you observe him rubbing his forehead. Based on visual observation alone, you might conclude that he is angry with you. But your perception may not be accurate. You truly do not know exactly what he is feeling. And so you ask. In a non-judgmental manner you state your observation and offer an interpretation of what it might be, and then ask for clarification. For example, you can say, "I see you rubbing your forehead. I'm wondering if you are angry with me. Am I right?" Of course your intuition may be correct, but it also may be wrong. Your husband, instead, may be rubbing his forehead out of utter shame and embarrassment. If the conversation had continued with you believing that he was angry, the direction of the conversation may have taken a turn for the worse.

A key component to the perception check is the admission that you may or may not be accurate in your perception. You need to be able to communicate your perception without declaring the presumption that you have already reached the conclusion that it was accurate. The words you use are exceptionally important. The most effective perception checks begin with phrases such as: "I get the impression that…" "It seems to me that…" "I'm wondering if…" "It sounds to me as if…" "Is it possible that…" "I get the feeling that…"

After you state your observations, be sure to ask a question, so that your partner knows that you do not presume to be omniscient and you realize your perception may be in accurate. Effective perception checks are followed with questions such as: "Am I right?" "Is that correct?" "Is this how you feel?" "Is that true for you?" Keep in mind that there is no way for you to know with absolute certainty what the other person is thinking or feeling. You need to ask.

Time Out: When there is a conversation involving heightened emotion, one of the most beneficial interventions that couples can utilize is a "time out." This means that at any point in the conversation, either party has the right to request a time out at which point the conversation comes to an end. Especially when the conversation becomes unproductive, there needs to be a way to bring the conversation to temporary closure. But the key is "temporary." Whether the person requests five minutes, thirty minutes, several hours, or a day, the intention is to keep the conversation productive. It is not a way to getting-in the last word or cutting-off your partner who is saying something you do not want to hear. Neither is it a time to step away from the conversation in order to re-group and develop a new strategy in order to "win" the argument. If that is the intention, then a time-out would be nothing less than manipulation. Instead, the intention of a time out is to allow each person time to focus attention on resolving the issue at hand.

The person making the request for a "time out" must be specific about how much time is being requested. For example, "I need a time out. Let's take five minutes (or an hour or a day)." After that time is up, the person who made the request must return to the partner to reinitiate the conversation. A couple can take as many time outs as needed. If respectful of one another, couples can utilize this technique as a primary tool to transform potentially hostile arguments into productive, solution-focused conversations.

A WORD FROM STEVE

Dear Jan,

I don't know if you realize it, but today is an anniversary, of sorts. It was exactly a year ago that you discovered me at the computer. It was the worst day of my life. But in a strange way, it was also the best. I will never ever forget the disappointment on you face when you walked in on me. And I will also never forget your courage to force me to face up to what I was doing to myself (and to you). For too long I was too afraid to face up to the truth about myself. And you, my sweet bride, had the courage to confront my problem.

When I look back at the changes in our marriage in this past year, I can't help but feel glad for the changes we have made. Our communication is better (way better) and I feel as if I understand you and you understand me like never before.

Thank you, Jan. For everything.

Love, Steve

Can You Forgive Me?

On Forgiveness and Reconciliation

KATHY AND TOM'S STORY

I had long suspected that Tom was using the computer to look at pornography, but every time I confronted him he assured me that nothing was going on and that I was just being paranoid and distrusting. There was one occasion when I checked the computer history and discovered that he had gone to some pornographic Web site. When I asked him about it he told me that some guy from the office had sent him something as a joke. He acted as if he was deeply offended and morally outraged that his friend would do such a thing. He said he didn't want to tell me because he didn't want me to be upset.

That is what he said, but deep in my heart I knew it wasn't true. He lied to me.

I know this because I walked in on him and saw for myself exactly what he was doing. He was sitting there at the computer looking at an incredibly graphic picture. And he was masturbating.

It was bad enough to have walked in on him, but his reaction actually made me hurt even more. He suggested that I was overreacting. He said things like, "It didn't mean anything" and "I didn't mean to hurt you" and "This wasn't about you, it was about me" and

"It doesn't mean I don't love you, or want you" and "It doesn't mean anything is wrong with 'us.'"

All I could do was stand there and cry.

He slept on the couch that night. And the next day we didn't talk about it. Actually, we didn't talk about it for days. Days of silence between us. I wanted to know what was going on with him, but I was afraid to ask. Maybe I was afraid of the answer.

After several frustrating days of not dealing with this issue, Tom finally broke the silence. He came home early from work and told me he had a confession to make. He told me he had a problem with looking at pornography on the computer. He said he wanted to stop, but it was like he couldn't help himself. He said he didn't mean for this to ever be a problem, but over time, he became more consumed with it.

He asked me to forgive him.

Of course I said yes. It is what I was supposed to do. He said he was sorry. I could see the regret and remorse on his face. There was sadness in his eyes. What else was I supposed to say but, yes, I'd forgive him.

But that didn't make the pain and confusion go away.

Over the next few months, I struggled with trying to understand Tom's desire for pornography. I wanted to be supportive of him, but I couldn't help but feel angry, sad, and resentful. I was angry at Tom and at our culture that seems so preoccupied with sex. I was sad that something might be wrong with our marriage; sad that he might not find me attractive anymore. And even though Tom finally admitted he had a problem, I still resented that he had lied to me all those times.

I tried to talk to Tom about how I felt, but it was as if my feelings fell on deaf ears. He would have glazed-over look in his eyes, like he was looking at me but not listening. Over and over he would tell me that he was sorry but didn't know what else to say. And so after a while he said nothing at all, telling me that I had to get over it.

It made me wonder if he even cared. It was depressing. I cried myself to sleep many nights. I knew he heard me, but why didn't he do or say anything? Why not just touch me on the shoulder and let me know everything would all be ok? Just say or do something!

I just wish he would understand what this has been like for me. Doesn't he care that I lay awake at night worrying if our marriage will survive? Doesn't he notice that I have felt so sick over this that I am hardly eating? Does he realize that this is about me too?

Despite Tom's reassurances that he would not look at pornography again, the trust had been broken. I said I forgave him, but I wonder if I really ever did. My feelings were like a mixture of guilt and anger: guilt that I can't seem to forget what he had done; anger because it seems so unfair that I even have to deal with something that I'm not responsible for.

He asked me to forgive him and I said I did. But why can't I forget? Why can't I get over this?

Cybersex: A Breach of Fidelity

"I didn't mean to hurt you." "This wasn't about you, it was about me." "It doesn't mean I don't love you, or want you." "It doesn't mean anything is wrong with 'us.'"

These are typical reactions from husbands offering assurance to their wives that their cybersexual behavior has minimal effect on their marriage. These sorts of comments are not surprising, since most men who use cyberporn actually believe that their behavior has little to no negative effect on their lives or relationships. But these comments stem from a perception wherein they consider the use of pornography to be "recreational." Their wives' perception, however, is radically different. Wives consider the use of pornography to be a breach of trust in the marital relationship.

In the year 2000, there was an extensive research study of 9,265 people who admitted to using the computer to view pornography or engage in cybersex. Participants in this study responded to an online survey posted on the MSNBC website over a seven-week period. In this study, two questions examined how pursuing online sexual materials may have interfered with or jeopardized certain aspects of respondents' lives. Overall, 32% of the entire sample identified at least one area of their life that has been negatively affected by their online sexual pursuits. When asked about jeopardizing a life area, 21% of all respondents reported that their online activities had jeopardized an area of their life. Interference was most reported in their personal life and relationships was the most common area jeopardized by online sexual pursuits.[1]

While the MSNBC study suggests that the majority of cybersex participants did not experience negative effects, there was another research study that focused on the wives and partners. In this study, conducted by Dr. Jennifer Schneider, one hundred percent of the respondents had experienced serious adverse consequences of their partner's cybersex involvement.[2] Her research determined that cybersexual behavior has profound effects on intimate relationships, including:

- Issues of trust and decreased intimacy were key factors in relationships problems.
- Being lied to repeatedly was a major cause of relational discord.
- Cybersex was a major contributing factor to separation and divorce.
- Two-thirds of couples experienced a serious decline in sexual relations as a result of one partner's cybersex involvement.
- Sixty-eight percent of couples lose interest in relational sex.
- Over fifty percent of those who turned to the virtual world to explore pornography and sex showed a decreased interest in sex with their real-life partner.
- Thirty-four percent of the partners were less interested in sexual intimacy knowing that their significant other was engaged in online sexual activity.

■ As a consequence of cybersex, some couples had had no relational sex in months or years.

Dr. Schneider also explored the effect of a parent's cybersexual behavior on children. Her research documented that the primary effects include:

■ An increased chance of exposure to computer-based pornography;

■ Involvement in parental conflicts.

■ Lack of attention because of one parent's involvement with the computer and the other parent's preoccupation with the cybersex addict.

■ Breakup of the marriage.

The Importance of Validation

When there has been a break in the relationship due to cyber-porn or cybersex, the husband must come to terms with the effect his behavior has had on his wife. He needs to understand that when his wife becomes aware of what he has been doing, she experiences a vast array of emotions, including feelings of hurt, abandonment, betrayal, rejection, loneliness, shame, humiliation, jealousy, anger, and loss of self-esteem. These are very real feelings that deserve validation. And when husbands dismiss or minimize these feelings by suggesting that the wife is overreacting, it only adds insult to injury.

Wives experience a variety of thoughts and feelings when encountering their husband's use of Internet pornography. Common reactions include:

■ "I don't really know what emotion to feel right now. I'm just numb all over."

■ "I don't know if I should cry, get mad, yell, or hit him."

■ "What did I do wrong? Maybe this is all my fault."

- "Should I leave him? Kick him out? Make him sleep on the sofa? I'm so confused, I don't know what to do or who to turn to right now."

- "Should I tell my parents? Should the kids know what's going on?"

- "I'm scared. I feel like my world is falling apart."

- "How could he do this to me? I thought we had a good marriage."

- "How can I compete with all those young women? My butt is bigger, my breasts are sagging, and I've given birth to children. I'm not twenty anymore!"

- "What else he is hiding or what else has he done? I'm afraid there's another secret he hasn't told me about."

- "I don't know if I can ever forgive him. This just hurts so deeply."

- "Maybe I can forgive him over time, but I'll never forget."

- "I thought we had a good sex life. What am I doing wrong?"

- "Does he love me anymore?"

- "Why couldn't he come to me and tell me about this problem?"

- "Have the kids seen any of these pictures on the computer? I'm afraid to ask them."

- "I feel like a victim. I've done nothing wrong to deserve this."

- "Why did God let this happen to my marriage?"

It takes time to understand and sort out all these thoughts and feelings. For some wives, it can take years to cope with something that is so emotionally painful and traumatic. For others, the process can move along more quickly. Each person is unique, and moves along at her own pace. What is important is for women to know that they are not alone; that their thoughts and feelings are similar to those of other wives who have experienced their husband's cyber-infidelity. And it is critically important for men to understand, fully, the depth of pain that their wives are experiencing because of their choice to use Internet pornography.

A Break In the Covenant Relationship

The covenant relationship of marriage involves emotional and sexual loyalty. At the marriage altar, Christian couples enter a relationship pledging vows of fidelity and unconditional love. But what is a Christian couple to do when the vow of loyalty has been breached as one partner has strayed into the world of cyberporn and cybersex? Although men most often consider the behavior to be meaningless and devoid of emotional intimacy, their wives consider the behavior to be a bona fide form of infidelity. Even though there has been no "real" contact, wives consider their husbands' online sexual experience to be just as emotionally painful as real affairs. The sad reality is that not all Christian marriages can survive the emotional turmoil associated with cyberporn. In fact, online sexual activity is increasingly cited as reasons for divorce.[3]

A Christian couple, therefore, is faced with a dilemma. There has been a breach of infidelity, but there has also been a pledge to love one another without condition. It is in commitment to that covenant vow that couples should attempt to work through the often-difficult process of forgiveness and reconciliation. Not all couples, however, are capable of accomplishing this process due to an abusive, hostile relationship. If such is the case for you, we strongly encourage you seek pastoral guidance and counsel.

For some couples, the rupture in the relationship is one painful moment of discovery. The wife discovers something on the computer or actually walks in and catches her husband in the act. Immediately there is a confrontation and the process of healing begins. For others, though, the breach of promises has occurred on multiple occasions. Many times before there was the suspicion that something was wrong but when asked, their husbands offered excuses rather than confession. Others wives hear promises not to repeat the transgression only to discover later that the pledge had been broken again. Many times they have heard words of regret and promises to change, only to discover a continued pattern of betrayal.

Whether the transgression has been confronted immediately or over the course of time, couples face the difficult task of engaging in the process of forgiveness and reconciliation. But although this process is the hallmark of the Christian tradition, many in the faith community have never received training or specific guidance on how to accomplish genuine "forgiveness" and "reconciliation."

There are common misconceptions about forgiveness that compromise many couples' capacity to achieve reconciliation.[4] These misconceptions include:

- **Forgiveness means forgetting.** Not only is this impossible, but to forget may actually perpetuate the problem. Whenever there has been some violation in the marriage contract, the result will be some measure of pain. To forget that pain is fantasy. To forget is to pretend the pain was never there. The reality, though, is that the initial injury left an emotional scar. And that scar, as unfortunate as it may be, will serve as a reminder to not repeat the hurtful act.

- **Forgiveness means no consequences.** For a marriage partner to offer amnesty (which means to drop the charges, requiring no penalty, recourse, or punishment) is to take away from the wrongdoer the necessity of showing penance. For reconciliation to be complete, the wrongdoer must have an opportunity to demonstrate, by words and actions, a sense of regret and a desire to offer restitution.

▪ **Forgiveness is an event.** True forgiveness and reconciliation requires an enormous investment of emotional and spiritual energy and it is not likely to be accomplished in a brief period of time. The process itself is time-consuming, although there is no set, prescribed time-period. What some couples may be able to accomplish in a few hours may take other couples weeks or months. The issue is not so much the amount of time, but whether both partners are actively working toward forgiveness and reconciliation.

The Process of Forgiveness

In one of his books on forgiveness entitled *Forgive and Forget*, award winning author Lewis Smedes discussed the importance of moving from hurt and hatred to healing and reconciliation. He described how forgiveness was not an event, but a process. He emphasized that spiritual and emotional battles cannot be expected to be won instantly. Just as we would not expect a widow to accept immediately her husband's death without grieving, so we can't expect victims to forgive the wrong-doer immediately. The forgiveness cycle, like the grief cycle, must run its course before reconciliation can happen.

For Wives

For those who have been wronged, betrayed, or violated, there are (according to Lew Smedes[5]) four identifiable steps in the process forgiveness:

Recognize and admit that there is pain. When somebody causes you pain so deep and unfair don't pretend you don't suffer. Don't pretend the wrong doesn't matter. It does matter. Your husband has chosen to set his eyes on someone other than you, and his actions have cut you to the core.

Recognize the hate. Recognize the human instinct that when a person hurts you, you want that person to hurt. Instinctively, you want the offender to suffer as much as you have. You may not hate your partner, but you hate what he has done. But be careful because the hate (like radioactive nuclear waste) can turn its power in on itself - to destroy you. It will sap the energy of the soul, leaving it weaker than before, too weak to create a better life beyond the pain.

Recognize that there is healing. It is here that you recognize that you cannot change the past, but you can heal the hurt that comes to you from the past. It is here that you recognize that the power-source for healing comes from outside yourself. It is here that you recognize that when Christ commands us to forgive; when he commands us to love our enemies, he gives along with that command the power to forgive, the power to love.

Recognize that there is reconciliation. There will come a time when you invite the offender back into your life. Because you will never forget the initial offense, life will never be the same. But, by the grace of God, your lives together could possible be even better than before.

For Husbands

For those who have violated the relationship by indulging in pornography, there are also four levels in the process of repentance (the peak of which is reconciliation):

Perception. This step stresses the importance of understanding the unfairness of what you did. No, you don't have to understand everything. You probably will never understand fully how hurt your partner is. No matter. Accept the verdict. Admit that what you did was thoughtless and selfish.

Pain. At this second level of repentance, you feel the pain that you inflicted. At the first step you articulated words. Now it is time to demonstrate that those words have meaning. Allow yourself to have these feelings, even if it feels bad to do so. Try not to deny or block out your feelings. It is important for your spouse to know you feel badly about what you have done.

Confession. To confess, in a spiritual sense, is not to merely admit that we did something wrong. To confess is to enter the heart of the person you hurt and to tell them that you hurt as they hurt. When you confess, you stand naked in the eyes of the one you hurt, pleading nothing but the hope of grace. This is the most difficult step. It is almost unbearable! For it is harder sometimes to confess to another human being than it is to confess to God.

Promise. This is the last step in the repentance process, the step that allows reconciliation to occur. Now that you know and feel the wrongness of what you did and have revealed your feelings to the one you offended, now you have a passionate desire not to hurt again. It is the desire to be trusted again. It is a commitment that you will be worthy of trust. Expressing the desire to change creates hope that change will occur.

Scripture Guidance
for Forgiveness and Reconciliation

Some time later, Jesus went up to Jerusalem for a feast of the Jews. Now there is in Jerusalem near the Sheep Gate a pool, which in Aramaic is called Bethesda and which is surrounded by five covered colonnades. Here a great number of disabled people used to lie – the blind, the lame, the paralyzed. One who was there had been an invalid for thirty-eight years. When Jesus saw him lying there and

*learned that he had been in this condition for a long time,
he asked him, "Do you want to get well?"*

*"Sir," the invalid replied, "I have no one to help me
into the pool when the water is stirred. While I am trying
to get in, someone else goes down ahead of me."*

*Then Jesus said to him, "Get up! Pick up your mat
and walk." At once the man was cured; he picked up his
mat and walked.*

JOHN 5:1–9, NIV

Do you want to get well? Do you want your marriage to get better? Do you want to work through the process of forgiveness and reconciliation?

This story from the Gospel of John offers spiritual wisdom to those who turn to Jesus for healing.

The event takes place at the pool of Bethesda. The gospel writer refers to all the people gathered there "disabled," and makes specific reference to them as blind, lame, or paralyzed. Amongst this group was one individual in particular who had been sick for thirty-eight years. He and the others were at the pool of Bethesda for a purpose. It was not just a place for disabled persons to congregate. It was a place full of symbolic meaning. It was a place where people looked for the Spirit of God to heal them.

This pool was located near the Sheep Gate on the northern side of the Jerusalem Temple. It was believed that on occasion an angel of the Lord stirred the waters in the pool and that the first person to step in after the angel had come would be healed. We can imagine that day after day, year after year this individual would sit near the pool waiting for the waters to be stirred by the healing power of God. And time and time again, others would reach the pool before him whenever the waters were stirred.

Clearly, this person hoped to be healed. He believed that God had the power to heal him. He only lacked the ability to enter the pool when the waters were stirred.

And Jesus approached this person and asked, "Do you want to get well?"

He responded by pointing out to Jesus the predicament he was in; that he had no one to help him into the pool when the healing waters were stirred. In a sense he was communicating a sense of futility, that he would forever be held captive by his condition and situation. Although he came to the pool wanting to be healed, he wasn't sure how that healing could come to be.

And that is how it is for many couples whose relationships have been torn asunder by cyberporn. Having experienced a breach of fidelity in the relationship, many couples are wounded by the transgression and do not know how to find healing. It is not a lack of belief in the power of God to heal the relationship. It is not a lack of belief that forgiveness is possible. It is being immobilized by the breach of trust.

Couples want to repair the relationship. They want to reestablish trust and commitment. They want to experience forgiveness and reconciliation. But feeling immobilized by the pain of their experience, they just do not know what to do.

And to these couples we can imagine Jesus would ask, "Do you want to get well?"

If so, "Get up! Pick up your mat and walk."

If you want your marriage to survive, if you desire forgiveness and reconciliation, there is something you must do: Trust in God enough to pick up the pieces of your broken relationship and get to the work of forgiveness.

Forgiveness and reconciliation don't just happen. It takes action on your part. It is more than attitude or a state of mind. There are tasks that must be done in order for forgiveness and reconciliation to occur.

And if doing something sounds strenuous, imagine what it must have been like for that man who had been paralyzed for thirty-eight years. He encountered Christ. He experienced divine healing.

But what about those whose relationships have been hurt, perhaps even paralyzed, by cyberporn? When it comes to forgiveness, how do you "stand up, take your mat, and walk?"

Consider this parable:

> *If your brother sins against you, go and show him his fault, just between the two of you. If he listens to you, you have won your brother over. But if he will not listen, take one or two others along, so that `every matter may be established by the testimony of two or three witnesses.' If he refuses to listen to them, tell it to the church; and if he refuses to listen even to the church, treat him as you would a pagan or a tax collector."*
>
> MATT. 18:15–20, NIV

This is a familiar passage of Scripture for those in the faith community. Christians are well familiar with the admonition to go and confront the person who has sinned against them in order to seek reconciliation. But for most it is an uncommon strategy. Instead, most wives who discover their husbands are using cyberporn react in one of three ways: the ostrich response, the passive-aggressive response; and revenge and retribution.

The Ostrich Response: Like an ostrich with its head in the sand, a confrontation is avoided. We pretend that nothing is wrong. We tell ourselves to forget it. To just let it go. That there is no need to get upset. That it's a "guy thing" to look at pornography.

With this approach, the reality is that as hard as you try to pretend that nothing is wrong, the harder it is to be around your husband. You just don't feel happy or content. You feel a chasm of emotional distance from him. But you tell yourself that this is better than a fight and that if you ignore it then maybe it will just go away.

The Passive-Aggressive Response: You tell yourself there is no need to confront him directly. You feel that intuitively he will come to realize that you are avoiding him and he will come to realize that you know something. He is wrong; you are right. And if you lay in bed like a cold fish then maybe it will get through his thick skull that you know what he has been doing and you disapprove.

Revenge and Retribution: Rather than confrontation, you take every opportunity to take get back at him for hurting you. He offended you, so you look for ways to offend him. You are angry that he is looking at airbrushed, perfect women and you take it upon yourself to point out his imperfections. You comment on his balding head or the spare tire around his waste. Or you comment on his age. Your comments are intended to cut him down and to make yourself feel better.

These are common strategies, but they fall far short of Jesus' expectations.

Looking at his words from the Gospel of Matthew, one of the most difficult aspects of Jesus' admonition is that he puts the burden of confrontation and confession on the person who has been hurt, wronged, or violated. It may not seem fair, but that is what Christ tells us to do. But notice something else in that passage. Jesus seems far less interested in who is right and who is wrong. His primary concern is on getting people who were in relationship and who have had a breach in that relationship find a way to work toward forgiveness and reconciliation.

When hurt and offended that your partner has used pornography or has used the computer to engage in cybersex, you have the right to be hurt and angry. No one should expect you to experience anything less. But what you do with those feelings can either destroy you and your relationship or it can serve as a motivator to muster up the courage to approach your partner and begin the work of forgiveness and reconciliation. But how?

Strategies for Forgiveness
and Reconciliation

The path to forgiveness and reconciliation is a journey that begins by taking one step at a time. When the bonds of marital trust are shattered and broken, this journey of healing is borne out of a crisis. A crisis of betrayal attacks the marital foundation at its very core. The earth may seem to shake, and the heavens rumble, and suddenly, the commitment and security one felt by making and taking their marital vows public and before God lie in pieces. Many couples wonder whether they can put these broken pieces of their marriage back together. There is confusion, hurt, sadness, anger; feelings that seem to suddenly appear, but don't fade away overnight. The situation may seem desperate, and even hopeless to some. Restoring hope can seem so distant when the painful wounds of betrayal are inflicted.

Some marriages can survive the crisis, and the marriage becomes stronger than ever. For others, the wounds are so deep, that the survival of the marriage is threatened. For some, the process of healing progresses along rather smoothly and quickly. For many, however, it takes time to heal, as each individual in the marriage must now confront many obstacles and hurdles. The emotional pain is real, and scary to face. Many questions and issues are now raised for perhaps the first time in the history of the marriage. Couples are confused how to take the first step in healing, and the journey seems like it will take place in uncharted waters. There may be marital problems which have developed and evolved over the course of the marriage that have never been addressed, or attempts at resolution have failed, causing a loss of faith and a fear of trying again. People lose faith in themselves, partners, and even God. They feel their prayers over the years have gone unanswered, and the core of ones faith is challenged. Individual also may bring problems starting in their childhoods into their marriages as well. Opening up old childhood wounds once thought healed surface once again.

As difficult as it may be, however, genuine forgiveness and reconciliation are possible.

Taking the Initial Steps

The first step in the forgiveness and reconciliation process is to trust and believe the relationship can be restored. A positive and believing attitude starts the journey on a positive note. It communicates an expectation that change will occur.

Secondly, begin the journey with prayer. Let God intervene right at the start. God already knows of the pain. He wants to help. Pray alone, pray with each other, and ask others to pray for you.

Third, recognize the common obstacles that prevent the forgiveness process from working. Clients at the Hope and Recovery Institute who struggled with forgiveness came to recognize factors that hindered their desire to achieve renewal in their relationships. Some of these obstacles include:

- A lack of faith that prayer really works.
- A belief that God has given up and abandoned the relationship.
- Denying the problem. Avoiding the problem. Minimizing the impact of the problem on self and family.
- Feeling unsafe to express real feelings with partner, fearing it will cause ones partner to relapse.
- Pride. Being too hesitant to turn to others for help.
- Making promises to stop engaging in online sexual activity and then repeatedly breaking the promise.
- Failure to take responsibility for ones actions, and instead blaming others or situations for the problem.

- Poor communication between partners.

- Not spending enough time working to save the relationship.

- Intense, unresolved anger.

It's important for couples to think about and reflect on the obstacles that might hinder renewal and restoration of the relationship. Husbands and wives need to be honest and open with themselves and with each other. Sometimes, it can be very insightful to ask your spouse what they see as a potential obstacle for you. This is risky. Sometimes feelings can be hurt, and you can be shocked by what your spouse may say. But then again, who will know you any better than your spouse. The tendency is to feel a bit resistant when we are told about our faults. It's natural to feel some defensiveness. But if this form of sharing and communicating is done with a loving and caring attitude, the walls of resistance often begin to tumble down. Insights and revelations about oneself begin to evolve, and this knowledge can go along ways toward healing the relationship.

> *"To forgive is to set a prisoner free—*
> *and discover that the prisoner was you."*
>
> LEW SMEDES

Forgiveness as a Reciprocal Process

Beverly Flanigan is another author who has written about forgiveness.[6] She developed what is known as the "Transactional Model of Forgiveness." This model is helpful in understanding how Christian couples can follow Christ's admonition in the eighteenth chapter of Matthew.

The key premise of Flanigan's transactional model is that every relationship has rules. Some rules are unspoken, but these rules are present and affect the relationship in some way. She suggests that early on in relationships people begin to establish rules, for example a rule regarding honesty and truthfulness. If you break something that belongs to you spouse or friend that is important to him, do you tell the truth or make up some excuse? In another example, if you spouse gets a new hairstyle that she really likes but you dislike, do you share your opinion or just agree with her? There are various "rules" in relationships and they are not exactly the same for all relationships.

Whether spoken or unspoken, every couple has developed some "rule" regarding the use of pornography and cybersex. If the rule establishes that this type of activity is not acceptable, then engaging in such activity is a violation of the rule in the marriage. Consequently, an injury to the relationship occurs, and trust has been broken.

Flanigan's forgiveness model emphasizes that forgiveness and reconciliation is a reciprocal process wherein both parties have an active role. To achieve genuine forgiveness and reconciliation, both parties must be involved. Both parties must recognize the violation. Both feel bad, but the injurer feels particularly guilty. All the while, though, both continue to believe that the "rule" between them was, and still is, good. One party made a mistake, that's all. However painful the mistake might be, both people want to adhere again to the original rule they developed together. The contrite member can apologize and make promises. In response, the violated person can condemn or even punish the offender. In the end, apologies are accepted. The anger passes, and both people voluntarily agree to commit themselves to their original rule about how they should treat each other. They may even decide to change the rule a little; but both people agree to abide by that rule.

The model diagramed in Table 4-A illustrates the transactional or reciprocal nature of forgiveness and reconciliation. In marriage relationships, both partners have an active role. The process begins with a confrontation. The offended spouse must have the courage to confront the partner (see chapter 3). The pornography-user must allow himself to be held accountable. At this stage in the process husband and wife must spend considerable time in conversation discussing the nature of the offense and identifying what "rules" in the relationship have been broken as a consequence. Failure to adequately identify the rule will derail the forgiveness/reconciliation process. The offended spouse must be able to verbalize and articulate the reasons why the behavior was wrong while the partner

TABLE 4-A

A Transactional Model of Forgiveness and Reconciliation[7]

OFFENDED SPOUSE	PORNOGRAPY-USER
Accuses the porno-user of violating a relationship rule	Apologizes for breaking the rule
Summarizes the reasons the behavior was wrong	Listens and accepts
Expresses rage, sorrow, and a desire to punish the porno-user	Accepts this punishment
Seeks assurance the offense will not be repeated	Promises to never repeat the offense
Accepts promises and demands no further "payment of debt"	Trusts that forgiveness is permanent
Recommitment to re-established or new rules	Recommitment to re-established or new rules

engages active listening skills. The partner must resist defensiveness and focus on understanding how the online sexual activity affected the other.

On a visual diagram, the process may appear mechanical and void of emotion. On the contrary, though, when forgiveness and reconciliation is a reciprocal process, it is imperative that the couple permits (and encourages) the healthy expression of emotion. As described earlier in this chapter, wives experience a wide range of emotions when they discover that their husbands are using Internet pornography. The husband must allow the wife to express these feelings. The pornography-user, though, also is experiencing emotions and those too must be expressed. Couples may need to seek professional guidance if both parties are experience deep resentment or rage. But where this transactional model is most effective is when the pornography-user comes to fully comprehend the nature of the offense and express true contrition, guilt, and sorrow for the behavior.

The goal of this transactional/reciprocal model is the reestablishment of trust. A relational rule has been broken and the couple must work collaboratively to either recommit to the rule or establish a new rule to put in its place. Reciprocally, wives and husbands must seek assurance and offer promises that the offense will not be repeated. Collaboratively, wives and husbands must covenant with each other that behavior in the future will be radically different, and trust that the forgiveness is permanent.

Action Steps in the Reciprocal Process

To forgive and to reconcile are verbs and as such are "action words" requiring people to engage their emotional and spiritual energy to heal and save the relationship. Each partner plays a critical role in making this happen. Let's take a look at important actions that will facilitate this process.

The Wife

1. Pray for your husband and yourself every day. Pray for renewed trust. Pray for honesty and openness

2. Be patient. Change takes time, especially if the problem is deep seated and serious. Sometimes relapse is a part of recovery. This is not an excuse to repeat the offense, but you have to be realistic. Some problems take time to fix. Try to be understanding, even though it may hurt to hear of a relapse. You need to communicate to your husband what form of a relapse is totally unacceptable. Working toward reconciliation is about facing reality, not denying it.

3. Expect your husband to change. He must clearly hear from you that you expect him to change. Be loving, but also firm.

4. Give yourself permission to have your feelings. You have a right to your feelings. They are yours. Feelings are normal. If you have been hurt, then you have a right to feel hurt. If you are angry, it's ok to be angry. Let your feelings out, and don't bottle them up inside. Don't be ashamed or embarrassed to have and express your feelings. Cry them out if you need to. Let your husband know exactly how you feel. It's very important he clearly understands the depth of the pain that has been caused. This can help prevent him from acting out again.

5. Give yourself permission to take your time to heal as well. Recovery is often focused on the husbands "problem" and wives are left out of the healing process. This leads to isolation and puts one at risk for depression. Find trusting people you can talk to about how you are doing as well.

6. Try to understand and recognize you might need to make some changes in the marriage as well. Listen to your husbands concerns. Talk about concerns with an attitude of openness. Work together and support each other in every step of this journey.

The Husband

1. Take responsibility for your actions and communicate clearly to your wife what it is that you are apologizing for. Avoid ifs, ands, or buts. The process of forgiveness and reconciliation will be derailed if you use language that shifts blame or responsibility onto your wife. The word "if" is particularly damaging. For example, saying "I'm sorry if this upset you" does very little to encourage forgiveness. You are implying that you do not know whether or not you did anything wrong. The word "but" also confounds the problem because it declares that anything you said before was meaningless. For example, if you say, "You know I love you and prefer to be with you and I know I shouldn't have looked at those pictures but I was horny and you didn't want to have sex." The word "but" is a clear signal to your wife that perhaps you are trying to affix blame on her and that you may not be as loving as loyal as you suggest.

2. Pray for your wife's healing as well as your own. Pray that you may be able to help her to trust you again. Recognize your wife is going through recovery just like you. Be patient with her. Ask her what she needs from you to be able to rebuild trust. Communicate directly and don't dance around the issues.

3. Remember those sayings like "The proof is in the pudding" or "Actions speak louder than words"? It works

this way in recovery, too. Forgiveness is more likely to occur when your wife sees you making real changes. This can be a change in the way you act or talk to her. The best way to build forgiveness is to put your wife's needs before your own. Demonstrate sincere repentance by explaining to her how you are going to change your attitudes and behaviors in the future. Give her specific examples, like "I will make sure I have deleted

Depression and Anxiety Take Their Toll

Depression and anxiety are the most common emotional states reported by women upon the discovery of marital infidelity, including the discovery that their husbands have breached the marriage covenant on the Internet. Whether viewing pornography or engaged in an "online affair," the reaction to the indiscretion and infidelity often leads to mood and anxiety disorders.

The National Institute of Mental Health has identified key symptoms that indicate the presence of depression and/or anxiety.[8]

Warning Signs of Depression

- Persistent sad, anxious, or "empty mood" feelings of hopelessness, pessimism
- Feelings of guilt, worthlessness, helplessness
- Loss of interest or pleasure in hobbies and activities that were once enjoyed, including sex
- Decreased energy, fatigue, being "slowed down"
- Difficulty concentrating, remembering, making decisions
- Insomnia early-morning awakening, or over sleeping

all pornography on the computer, every picture," or "I've changed my computer screen name so the people I have previously chatted with will no longer be able to contact me. I'm breaking off all relationships I developed while online." Remember, relationships and feelings are very fragile. No one likes to get his or her feelings hurt or have trust undermined. If you make a promise to change, then you must do your best to

- Appetite and/or weight loss or overeating and weight gain
- Thoughts of death, or suicide; suicide attempts
- Restlessness, irritability
- Persistent physical symptoms that do not respond to treatment, such as headaches. digestive disorders, and chronic pain

Warning Signs of Anxiety

- Persistent worrying. The worrying can be accompanied by physical symptoms such as fatigue, headaches, muscle tension, irritability, twitching, sweating, and hot flashes.
- Repeated and intense episodes of fear accompanied by physical symptoms such as chest pain, heart palpitations, shortness of breath, dizziness, or abdominal distress
- Overwhelming anxiety and excessive self-consciousness in everyday situations. A fear of being watched or judged by others in social situations. Fearful of being humiliated by one's own actions.

honor this commitment. Broken problems create doubt and anger, and after awhile, defensive walls will go back up, and loss of hope will creep in.

4. Remember your marital vows. They were made for a reason. Go back and look at the vow you made to your wife. This can help reinforce the commitment you made to her. It can help remind you why you married her in the first place. It can help put the relationship back in focus. She loves you more than any pornographic image you have ever looked at. She's your life partner.

5. Talk to your wife about your feelings. Many husbands struggle to talk about feelings. But many wives truly appreciate the husband who takes the time to talk to them. It's a way of expressing care and concern. It will make your wife feel you care about her when you trust her with your feelings. Let her know about the good days you are having and the battles you have won. Talk to her about any struggles to give in to the temptation of pornography. Be honest and sincere. Ask her how she is feeling about the progress you are making. Ask her how she is coping, and listen carefully to her response. She needs to be able to talk to you and express herself as well. Communication needs to be a two way street. Mutual sharing will help rebuild trust.

6. Talk to your pastor. Go to professional counseling. Share in a support group or men's Bible study. It is important to develop a network of people you can talk with and help hold you accountable for change. It is healthy to reach out to others who are supportive. Many men can relate to your struggles. Wives feel better when they see their husbands reaching out for help. Try to overcome the feeling you have to fix the prob-

lem yourself. You need more than your wife to count on for support. It's not her role to act like a police officer and spy on you. She's trying to understand and work through her own feelings as well as trying to understand yours. A humbling approach will go along ways toward rebuilding trust.

AN UPDATE ON KATHY AND TOM

Kathy and Tom made very good progress in reconciling their relationship. Kathy worked very hard to forgive Tom while he worked to regain her trust. There were days of tension and even self-doubt, but they made a commitment to change, trusted God, and celebrated successes together. Tom was still tempted from time to time to return to pornography. Once in awhile he slipped up and looked at pornography on the Internet. He felt badly, told Kathy of his relapse, and they prayed each time for healing. Tom knew he would be tempted, but each time he resisted, he grew stronger and the grip of pornography weakened.

They both identified obstacles to change right at the beginning. For Tom, he was a proud man, but was humbled when his secret was out. When confronted by Kathy, he apologized. They both had many feelings. Tom felt ashamed and embarrassed. He knew he violated the marriage covenant. It took him time to understand and express these feelings to Kathy, and he shared one feeling at a time. Kathy worked hard to understand and overcome her anger, and in time, her hurt and anger began to subside. Tom became a better listener and was able to grasp the depth of Kathy's emotional pain. She appreciated being able to express her feelings to Tom without him becoming angry with her. Together, they worked at trusting God, and began to spend more time nurturing their relationship. These steps proved helpful to them to move beyond the pain to experiencing genuine forgiveness and reconciliation.

5

What Were You Thinking?

A Question of Repentance

TOM'S STORY

I grew up with pornography. My friends in high school all looked at dirty magazines. And my own dad had subscriptions to both *Playboy* and *Penthouse*. In a way I just figured that it was "normal" and I never considered pornography to be a big deal. At least not until now.

As I am writing this, I am sitting in my new one-bedroom apartment. I am alone and wondering what my wife and three children are doing back at home. Oh, how I wish I were with them. How I wish I could go back in time and undo all my stupid mistakes. How I wish I had thought more clearly of what I was doing that got me into this mess.

It was my fourteen-year-old daughter who actually made the discovery. The laptop I had purchased for the kids to use for their homework had crashed and, facing a deadline for a school project, she used the computer in my home office. It was while looking for some clip-art that she discovered my collection of pornography. She found not just one or two pictures. How many pictures there were, I'm not really sure. I don't think I could even count the number of pictures that I had downloaded over the years. And these were not just pictures of scantily clad women. The stuff I looked at was hardcore.

My sweet little girl realized within seconds that her dad was sick. Sick and perverted. And she hasn't spoken to me since.

I can still hear my wife's voice echo in my mind as she berated me: "What were you thinking?"

The reality is, I wasn't thinking. I wasn't thinking about the reality of what I was doing and how my behavior would affect my marriage or my family. And I definitely gave no thought as to how it would affect my relationship with God.

I have used pornography since I was a teenager. My wife didn't approve, so I couldn't subscribe to magazines like my father had done. Instead, I used the Internet. I would spend at least two hours a day surfing through porn sites and finding chatrooms to meet people to "trade" pictures with. Typically, I would wait until the kids had gone to bed and my wife was watching TV. I would tell her I needed to go upstairs and use the computer for work. Some of the time I actually had work to do, but that was more of a rare occasion. It got to a point when I considered this to be my "private time." With the kids asleep, the wife tired and preoccupied with the television, it was the perfect opportunity to be alone. At first I felt really guilty about lying to my wife, but over time the guilt was displaced by the thought that I deserved some private time.

When we first got the Internet, I never looked at porn sites when the family was around. But as time went on, I began to take a few more chances with them around. Initially, I was always sure that the door was closed, but after a while I wouldn't bother. I would just listen carefully for anyone coming up the stairs. I got very good at hiding the pornography if I thought there was a chance I could get caught. It was sort of like a game. And I grew ever more confident in my ability to keep it all a secret. Of course there was the chance of getting caught, but the risk made the game more exciting. It was being naughty, taking chances, and getting away with something.

Like many men, I tricked myself into believing what I was doing wasn't that bad. I used to tell myself that I wasn't really hurting anyone. I figured I didn't really know these girls personally. If they were in these types of pictures without their clothes on, then that was their choice. They must really want to be seen this way or they wouldn't do it. After all, they were adults. No harm, no foul. Besides, my wife wouldn't dress the way they did. I tried to get her to dress the way I thought was sexy, and she wouldn't do it. So I figured that if my wife wouldn't dress or act like them that there wasn't any harm in just looking at a few pictures now and then, pictures of women who seemed so willing and confident.

I didn't really feel like I was cheating either. I told myself over and over again that it was just for fun. The more I told myself this, the more I believed it. It was like I eventually convinced myself what I was doing was acceptable.

There were some times when I thought I was losing control and would make a decision to stay away from the computer. But that would last not more than a week or so. I found myself thinking about pornography a lot when I was home, at work, and sometimes even while at church. My mind would wander during the pastor's sermon. I'd think about when the next opportunity would present itself. I know it sounds crazy, but it's true. What was I thinking?

I wasn't thinking about my wife. I wasn't thinking about my children. I wasn't thinking about God. I wasn't thinking I had a problem.

But I did. And as a result I lost my family.

Stinking Thinking Makes for Rotten Relationships

In many ways, human behavior is the result of what people think or believe about themselves and others. Our thoughts, beliefs, assumptions, and expectations direct how we behave. When our thoughts are rational (that is to say, accurate), we behave in rational ways. For example, when a husband attempts to initiate sexual intimacy and is told by his wife that she has a headache, his brain immediately begins to sort through lots of information: she has a history of migraines; migraines seem to run in her family; when she gets a migraine she feels sick to her stomach; what she needs is peace and quiet; the migraines never seem to last more than a day or two. With this information, the husband rationally takes action. He offers to call the doctor; he makes sure she is comfortable; he makes sure the kids are playing quietly. But the interaction between husband and wife could become severely distorted if there is a faulty or irrational thought process. If he believes that she is just being avoidant; if he interprets her response to be an indication that she is "frigid" and uninterested in sex; if he believes that she does not enjoy moments of physical and sexual intimacy, the entire scenario could become explosive.

God has created humans with the capacity to think. We have the ability to reason, solve problems, and examine issues from various points of view or perspectives. By divine design humans have the wonderful ability to stop our thoughts in midstream to correct our assumptions, beliefs, or expectations. And in correcting the thought process, humans have the capacity to alter their behavior. When faced with a problem situation, human beings have the capability to think about the nature of the problem and consider a multiplicity of ways to resolve the situation. And it is all by God's design.

In the 1950s, psychologists such as Albert Ellis and Aaron Beck came to discover the importance of irrational or faulty thinking and its effect on human behavior.[1] Based on vast empirical research, psychologists utilize a method of intervention known as "cognitive behavioral therapy" to assist people with their problems. Initially used as a treatment model for depression, cognitive behavioral therapy (also known as CBT) has been applied to help people cope with (and change) a wide variety of problems in life, including problems associated with online sexual activity and sexual addictions.

The CBT model works on a very important principle, that thoughts, belief systems, and assumptions affect human emotions and behavior. The primary goal of CBT is to help people identify irrational, inaccurate, faulty, or destructive thought patterns and replace them with alternative thoughts which are more positive, realistic, and healthy. This is more complicated than just developing a "positive thinking" approach of "looking on the bright side." It entails learning to identify the "stinking thinking" and discover alternative, more realistic, rational interpretation.

Sometimes, people are consciously aware of their thoughts and perspectives. Others are unaware how their thought processes impact their emotional life and decision-making. Many people who struggle with pornography are oblivious to how their faulty thought process fuels their cybersexual behavior. Three of the most common, and by far the most dangerous, erroneous thoughts include minimization, justification, and musterbating.

Minimization

Perhaps the most foul and stinky of all irrational thoughts in regard to pornography: "It's not that big a deal."

It *is* a big deal.

In the first place, pornography victimizes people. The vast majority of pornography depicts people engaged in sexual experiences that appear to be consensual. The persons depicted seem to be enjoying the experience and appear comfortable with being filmed and photographed. The sad reality is that many of them are forced to participate, manipulated through drugs, or threatened with bodily harm if they do not participate.

Second, pornography affects marital relationships. According to research, most men do not believe that their use of pornography has had a negative effect on their relationships.[2] However, when researchers explored the wives' experience, 100 percent of them felt that their husbands' use of pornography had a harmful effect on the marriage.[3]

Third, pornography affects the individual. Research indicates that it is possible to develop an addiction to pornography. What may have started as mere recreational use becomes an obsession. Like a drug, the individual uses pornography more frequently than intended. The type of material viewed escalates from erotica to hardcore. In order to achieve the same level of sexual arousal as before the individual requires pornographic images that are increasingly more intense and graphic. The individual begins to disregard responsibilities at home or work while his time and energy are absorbed in the use pornography. The individual continues using pornography even though he recognizes that it is having a harmful effect on himself and his relationships.

Justification

Christians know that the use of pornography is inappropriate. They are well aware that the use of pornography is a sexual sin that dishonors God and distorts their relationship with God and can potentially distort their relationship with wife and family. But they continue to use it. The choice to use pornography is driven, though, by a negative thought process known as "justification." Justifications are excuses that echo inside a person's mind giving them an excuse to use pornography. The problem, however, is that in most cases the thought-process is faulty. In Tom's situation, he knew that porn was wrong, but he exercised very little self-control or restraint. He justified what he was doing by allowing irrational and incorrect thoughts to direct his use of porn.

Some of the more common justifications include:

- "It's not like I don't love my wife. It's just for fun."

- "I just need sex more than my wife does."

- "It's not as bad as guys who go to prostitutes."

- "It could be worse. I could be having a real affair."

- "If I was getting more sex at home, I wouldn't need to do this."

- "At least it's not kiddie porn."

- "It helps me relax."

- "I'm lonely and I get to talk with others who know what I'm going through."

- "I only look at pictures once a week; it's not like I have a real problem."

- "If I don't masturbate regularly, I feel like I'm going to explode."

Musterbating

No, it's not a typo. This is not about *masturbation*. This stinking-thinking process is about faulty expectations wherein a person's irrational beliefs put unreasonable demands on themselves and others. Albert Ellis calls this type of faulty thinking "musterbating."[4] People rationalize their use of pornography if they believe that their expectations are not being met. People who "musterbate" have thought processes which reflect a sense of what "must" or "should" be occurring in their sexual relationship. In a sense, they believe that there are certain rules in regard to sex. When the rules are not being followed, there is disappointment and frustration.

Couples need to discover what these rules are and determine whether there is common agreement or if the expectations are unreasonable. For example, a husband might believe that in a healthy marital relationship a man and a woman should make love three times per week. The wife, however, believes that in a healthy marital relationship the sexual contact should occur once per week. The issue, though, is not over who is right and who is wrong. They both have expectations and rules in regard to the frequency of sexual intimacy. However, if one or both of them maintains the position that their view is correct and the other's faulty, there is potential for conflict. If husband and wife are not able to communicate and come to an agreement, there will be unresolved conflict.

The use of pornography introduces and reinforces faulty expectations. By viewing pornographic material or participating in chatrooms or newsgroups, a person develops beliefs and attitudes regarding sex and sexuality. This information, though, is usually inaccurate and yet the individual develops a sense that what they are experiencing is normative. The individual develops beliefs about the "rules" of sex, and over time these beliefs become more solidified and inflexible. In pornography, for example, women are portrayed as being multi-orgasmic and insatiable in their sexual desire. As a man is repeatedly exposed to this depiction they develop a sense that his wife "should" have multiple orgasms and she "should" be interested in sex far more frequently. Similarly, a man who views pornography and experiences women crying out in orgasmic ecstasy develops a rule that this is the epitome of expressing sexual satisfaction. With such expectation, the husband will be disappointed if his wife's experience is more subdued.

Evaluating Tom's "Stinking Thinking"

Tom's story, at the beginning of this chapter, demonstrates how faulty assumptions about pornography and "stinking thinking" led to an escalation of sexually inappropriately behavior.

Tom's use of pornography was getting out of control. Over time, he began to desire more and more pornography. Looking at a few pictures no longer satisfied his desire and craving. In his mind, he needed more. It became difficult for him to stop himself and control this desire. He justified his actions, which led to lying to his wife about why he was going to the bedroom at night. Sometimes, he really planned on working on the computer. But more often than not, he used the work excuse to cover his tracks. He even started to tell his wife he needed to work on the computer several hours before he actually went to his bedroom. He was practicing deception and becoming more confident as he practiced it. He became "comfortable" in lying. Tom illustrates this process very well when he stated, "my confidence in hiding all this got better."

Tom's deception was very conscious. He began to lie, justify his lying, and tried to block out any guilt and shame. At first, this was hard to do. He felt very guilty. But like many men, Tom's use of pornography reached the point where it became obsessive. He found it very difficult to stop and get control of himself.

As Tom became "more comfortable" in surfing the Internet for pornography, he also took more chances. He began to look at pornography when his children were home, a boundary he previously was unwilling to violate. He convinced himself he would not get caught, and though he felt guilty knowing the children were upstairs in their rooms next to his room, he began to feel less guilty over time. He began to believe since he had never been caught, he had perfected his strategy quite well. He convinced himself the children would never walk in on him, and if they did, he strategically planned a response. He anticipated a problem, but rather than eliminate the behavior itself, he found ways to perpetuate his situation. He learned how to quickly cover up the pictures on the computer monitor so no one would know what he had been looking, only magnifying the risk that his behavior would escalate.

Feeling less guilty over time is a common dynamic in the escalation of this process. It's another example how justification or rationalization can deaden the feelings of guilt during the quest of fulfilling sexual desire. Tom felt some guilt when looking at pornography, but he compartmentalized it, or simply made the guilt go away for a while so he could complete the act. He told himself they were just pictures. He had convinced himself that it was normal for women to act and dress like the women in the pictures, and when his wife did not meet this expectation, he became angry with her and felt rejected. He turned to the pictures for comfort and pleasure. He made one excuse after another.

This is a common sequence of events for many men. Guilt usually follows the use of pornography, and sometimes even deters someone from looking at it for a period of time. Once the desire returns however, and grows in strength and power, justification returns, and the cycle is repeated. Sometimes this cycle or pattern is repeated over and over again within a very short period of time. For others, the pattern is less frequent. Instead of looking at pornography once a day, it's looked at for a couple of hours during the week. Regardless of the pattern established, the risk is the escalation will continue and the frequency of usage and hunger to feed the desire become more intense.

In Tom's case, his excitement for pornography waxed and waned. He began to escalate by going to pornography sites on a regular basis, identifying his favorite sites so he could go back over and over, collecting pictures, and then masturbating to them. When pornography was reinforced by the pleasure achieved thru masturbation and orgasm, his desire for this type of feeling and sensation became stronger. Even this wasn't quite enough for Tom, as he discovered chatrooms and started talking with others about fantasies he had about his wife and other people. Ultimately, he justified chatroom conversation as acceptable because he really didn't know anyone personally, and besides, other men chatted in explicit ways as well.

Tom knew his behavior was wrong. There were times his desire to stop was also very strong, and sometimes he would be win this battle. There were times he clicked on the computer, was tempted to go to a pornography site, but did not go. He felt relieved and good about this decision. He prayed for self-control. When attending church, he felt ashamed and guilt-ridden, often feeling the pastor's sermons on sin were directly meant for him. But like many good men of faith, sometimes problems can get out of control. The intensity of the escalation process catches people off guard. What appears as one small, harmless justification leads to a web of lies and secrecy. This process caught Tom off guard. It was like he was ambushed from behind. The destructive lure and power of pornography hit him when his guard was down. He was held captive.

Tom fought hard to face these issues and is stronger today than when he first discovered Internet pornography. He freely admits it is a tough battle to fight. Sometimes he's relapsed and used pornography again. He felt bad about each relapse, but had the courage to recommit to change. He was able to identify his thought patterns and assumptions about pornography and how they reinforced and escalated. This awareness and courage will help him in the fight to win this battle at some point, once and for all.

Scriptural Guidance for Repentance

On day Peter and John were going up to the temple at the time of prayer—at three in the afternoon. Now a man crippled from birth was being carried to the temple gate called Beautiful, where he was put every day to beg from those going into the temple courts. When he saw Peter and John about to enter, he asked them for money. Peter looked straight at him, as did John. Then Peter said, "Look at us!" So the man gave them his attention, expecting to get something from them.

Then Peter said, "Silver or gold I do not have, but what I have I give you. In the name of Jesus Christ of Nazareth, walk." Taking him by the right hand, he helped him up, and instantly the man's feet and ankles became strong. He jumped to his feet and began to walk. Then he went with them into the temple courts, walking and jumping, and praising God. When all the people saw him walking and praising God, they recognized him as the same man who used to sit begging at the temple gate called Beautiful, and they were filled with wonder and amazement at what had happened to him.

While the beggar held on to Peter and John, all the people were astonished and came running to them in the place called Solomon's Colonnade. When Peter saw this, he said to them: "Men of Israel, why does this surprise you? Why do you stare at us as if by our own power or godliness we had made this man walk? The God of Abraham, Isaac, and Jacob, the God of our fathers, has glorified his servant Jesus. You handed him over to be killed, and you disowned him before Pilate, though he had decided to let him go. You disowned the Holy and Righteous One and asked that a murderer be released to you. You killed the author of life, but God raised him from the dead. We are witnesses of this. By faith in the name of Jesus, this man whom you see and know was made strong. It is Jesus' name and the faith that comes through him that has given this complete healing to him, as you can all see.

Now, brothers, I know that you acted in ignorance, as did your leaders. But this is how God fulfilled what he had foretold through all the prophets, saying that his Christ would suffer. Repent, then, and turn to God, so that your sins may be wiped out, that times of refreshing may come from the Lord.

ACTS 3:1–19, NIV

The Book of Acts is perhaps one of the more neglected books of the New Testament. Most are familiar with the Gospels of Matthew, Mark, Luke, and John. We read the Gospels that tell of the events of Jesus' birth, ministry, death, and resurrection. And many of us stop reading the Bible at the conclusion of each of these four gospels, thinking in a way that is where the story ends, with Jesus' resurrection. But there is more to the story.

While the Gospels end with the stories of Jesus' resurrection, the Book of Acts begins and ends with stories of the ongoing miracle of the resurrection of others. To be sure, we do not have people raised from graves as was Jesus, but we have people raised from certain kinds of graves, nevertheless.

Just as the Gospels conclude with the message that crucifixion and death are not the final words, the Book of Acts proclaims that the power of resurrection, by the grace of the Holy Spirit, is still possible. Lameness, deafness, blindness, disease, and physical and mental disabilities are not the final words about life. Healing, health, strength, sight, and vitality are the final words. After his own victorious resurrection, Jesus offers the power of resurrection through his life-giving Spirit. It is God's intention to continue the process of resurrection so that in place of discouragement and defeat, people can turn their lives around and experience renewal. By the grace of Jesus Christ, you can experience new life.

But how? How might you experience the power of resurrection?

Insight is found in Peter's sermon to the crowd at Solomon's Portico in the Temple where he says, "Repent then, and turn to God so that your sins may be wiped out, that times of refreshing may come from the Lord."

And what does it mean to repent? It means to change. The key to resurrection and new life is change.

When the author of the Book of Acts described this event in Jerusalem he used one of the classic Greek words for repentance:

metanoia. This word for repentance literally means a "change of mind" or transformation of thought patterns. One of the first steps toward renewal and resurrection is a change in our ways of thinking.

The lame beggar in this passage in the Book of Acts had to change his way of thinking in order to experience renewal. We are told he had been lame from birth and that he was now about forty. Since wheelchairs had not yet been invented, he had to be carried wherever he wanted to go. Indeed, some friends apparently were in the habit of carrying him to the gate each morning so that he could beg for money.

This man's entire identity was shaped by his physical condition. He viewed himself as nothing more than a beggar. His physical condition made it difficult for him to conceive of himself as equal to others. But Peter and John saw more than that. When they came upon him at the Temple Gate, the man asked them for some spare change. While most others would have averted their eyes or deliberately avoided the encounter, Peter "fixed his gaze upon him," as did John. They saw this man as much more than a beggar. They saw beyond this man's physical limitations to see him as a human being, a child of God. And they were about to help him gain the same perspective.

"I have no silver and gold, but I give you what I have; in the name of Jesus Christ of Nazareth, walk." Peter took him by the hand, raised him up, and soon he was walking and leaping and praising God, entering the Temple with them to worship to the amazement of all.

Was the power of the resurrected Jesus still at work? Indeed it was, not only in healing his physical condition, but also in changing this man's way of thinking about himself and the world. This man was overjoyed to change his entire self-image to live life as a whole man, healthy and well. No longer thinking of himself as handicapped, he celebrated his renewal by leaping and jumping his way into the temple courts to worship God!

Those caught in the mire of pornography and cyber-sex are in many ways psychologically and spiritually handicapped. They have grown accustomed to think in certain ways. Caught in the deception and inaccuracy of their thoughts they are left lame and powerless over their desires. They consider themselves paralyzed and incapacitated in controlling their behavior.

This inaccurate self-perception is the result of inaccurate thoughts that people have allowed to echo within their minds. Thoughts such as "It's not really hurting anyone." "It's better to look at pictures than have a real affair." "Using pornography is not as bad as using prostitutes." "It's just for fun." "At least I'm not using kiddie porn." "It helps me relax."

Psychologically, these thoughts shape attitudes and behavior that are problematic, maladaptive, and perhaps pathological. As described above, many of these thoughts reflect minimization, justification, and faulty expectations. Repentance, therefore, begins with a change in thought process. There must be a thorough and honest evaluation of thoughts, beliefs, and expectations.

Repentance, however, means more than just a change of mind. To be complete, repentance also requires a change in one's behavior.

Unfortunately, we know little about the lame beggar after the healing incident except that he entered the Temple praising God. However, we can imagine that Peter and John would have advised him to live a productive life as a follower of Jesus Christ. Not only was he to change his way of thinking of himself, he was to change his behavior, his ways of acting and doing. He couldn't sit around the temple gate anymore looking for handouts. He had to change his daily routine. He had to change his way of living.

For Christians who have used pornography, a change in thoughts, beliefs, and expectations is essential. But in addition, there is a critical need to change their sexual behavior. For complete repentance, Christians need not only to harness their thoughts, but to control their behavior as well.

Christians need to approach their sexuality as a spiritual discipline. Unfortunately, though, our culture has trained people to falsely believe that humans have little control over urges and desires. Popular culture has conditioned people to believe that sexual fantasy and unbridled desire are part and parcel of being human. But the reality is that God gave you the power (and the freedom) to make choices. And it is for you to choose to engage your sexuality in the way God has intended. Sex is not "naughty" or ungodly. God created you a sexual creature that responds to physical beauty. But use your sexuality as a reflection of God intentions, celebrating and enjoying it rather than debasing it and reducing it to nothing less than lust.

As a spiritual discipline, you have to develop power over your sexual desires. Some people excuse their behavior by "thinking" that it is beyond their control, that the images are too provocative, too alluring, too tempting. And to a degree this is true. The images are powerful. The temptation is real. But the power is not beyond you. You can make choices and you are responsible for your own behavior. This is an important fact that must echo within your mind and soul: God has given you willpower and it is for you to exercise and utilize that will to resist sexual temptation.

The Book of Acts has only twenty-eight chapters, and the twenty-eighth chapter ends abruptly—as if the rest of the story is to be continued. And it has been for twenty centuries. The faith community is a continuation of the story of the ongoing power of God. It continues wherever people are open to God's Spirit, willing to be raised from the dead by the power of Christ, willing to repent, to change in thought, action, and expectation. Such persons are proof of the ongoing power of resurrection.

So What Do You *Think* about Pornography?

Every person who has Internet access must make a decision. Is the use of pornography right or wrong? Does it honor God? Does it help me in my life of discipleship? Does it help my relationships?

Fundamentally, every person needs to evaluate his or her thoughts in regard to Internet pornography. You need to make a value judgment about whether the use of pornography is morally right or wrong. If you consider the use of pornography to reflect moral and spiritual failure, you will be more hesitant to use pornography because you have already concluded that it is as wrong. You have made a value judgment. If you think pornography is acceptable or believe it's not that bad, you will probably be more tempted to give in and look at it when given the opportunity to do so.

How a person thinks about pornography can dramatically affect their desire to use it, or strengthen their willpower to resist it. For example, the use of cocaine can stimulate pleasurable sensations throughout the body. But most people just know this is wrong and should never be tried. They know it's wrong even before experimenting and taking a chance. They think it's wrong. They believe its wrong. They are convinced it's absolutely wrong. They have no temptation to use it. The result? They never try it, not even once.

The pornography industry has tried to normalize the use of pornography in society. They want you to believe that pornography is harmless and that there are benefits to its use. In many ways the industry has been successful in its efforts, with many believing that the use of pornography is a normal part of being a man. Members of the faith community, however, are encouraged to "think," reflect on, and examine the impact pornography has had on their lives. By challenging themselves to "think," persons in the faith community will be better prepared to resist the temptation to use pornography.

The Three-Second Rule

This is a simple procedure or tool you can use to control your thinking. Remind yourself you have about three seconds to identify, catch, and change your thoughts. It is vitally important to identify and catch any faulty thoughts as soon as possible. A single thought can then lead to a series of thoughts, and eventually, a sexual fantasy. The longer you think about or dwell on pornographic images, the stronger your desire to act out what you are thinking. As your desire grows, justification and minimization will also occur. Like pouring gasoline on a fire, making excuses for your behavior will cause you to lose control of yourself. It is important to keep in mind that it doesn't take men very long to develop a very graphic and arousing sexual fantasy. It's harder to control one's sexual thoughts once these thoughts become arousing and pleasurable. Let's use Tom's situation to illustrate how the three-second rule might work for you.

When Tom was home at night with his family, he began to anticipate going upstairs and use the computer as soon as his children went to bed. This was a mental trigger to thinking about using pornography.

Tom would think to himself, "The kids are going to bed. This is my opportunity to use the computer and check my favorite porn site." As soon as he recognized he had this thought, he stopped it and changed it to, "This is time for me and my wife to spend together."

Here's another example. Tom was at work, daydreaming and thinking about the end of his workday. Out nowhere, Tom caught himself thinking, "Tonight I need some time to relax; I can't wait to get online." He countered this thought after recognizing it and then intervened by praying, "Dear Lord, deliver me from the desire to use pornography." Sometimes he would bring out his Bible at work and read a passage that was meaningful to him. This would immediately break the cycle of unhealthy thinking before he found himself drifting off into a sexual fantasy. This intervention works for many men.

When Tom overheard the guys at work talking about pornography, this triggered the thought, "See, it's normal; these guys do it." He countered the thought and replaced it with "It's wrong, I need to walk in the Spirit. I don't want to be like other guys."

Still, Tom found himself at times thinking, "I'm just so stressed out. I need a release." He countered this thought by telling himself, "I need to talk to my wife about my stressful day" or "I'm going to work out when I get home."

Whatever your situation might be, identify your most common thoughts or beliefs and write down a counter thought or belief like Tom did. It takes practice. The harder you try and the more you practice, you'll be able to catch your thoughts and replace them with something healthier under three seconds. If it takes longer than three seconds, that's OK. Try not to feel guilty or believe you are doing something wrong and failing. You'll get the hang of it with time, and you'll start to see the results. Remember, the goal is to identify unhealthy thoughts and replace them with more healthy and productive ones as soon as possible.

Thoughts and Counter Thoughts

Here are the most common thoughts, beliefs, and justifications people use when looking at pornography. Look at this list carefully and see if you can identify any of these in yourself or loved ones. Approach this list with an open mind. If you have identified some unhealthy thoughts on this list, examples are given how to replace destructive thoughts with healthier ones. These are called counter thoughts. You might come up with a better counter thought that is more suited to your situation which is great, because this is how you begin to challenge and attack your way of thinking. Replace the dysfunctional thought or belief with something more positive. Overtime, your pattern of thinking will change. You will feel better about yourself when your thoughts and beliefs are healthier.

Some examples of thought-substitution include:

Thought: I know it might be wrong, but I could be doing worse things. I could be drinking, staying out all night, or even having an affair.

Counter thought: There is no redeeming value in pornography. It does not honor God. It debases, rather than celebrates the God-given gift of sexuality.

Thought: Where do they find all those attractive women I see in the pictures and movies? They must really like sex!

Counter thought: There is no pleasure to be found knowing that many of the women in those pictures have histories of sexual abuse. Many are coerced to participate and others face severe physical abuse if they refuse.

Thought: Other guys look at this stuff. It must be pretty normal.

Counter thought: As a Christian, I am called to a high moral standard. I'm going to walk in the Spirit and strive to be a role model for others.

Thought: No one will find out. It's a secret.

Counter thought: It's NOT a secret. God knows.

Thought: If I were getting more sex at home, I wouldn't need this. I need some release.

Counter thought: Marriage is more than just sex. My spouse is my life partner. I need to talk to her about this aspect of our relationship.

Thought: It's true I masturbate while looking at pornography, but what guy hasn't?

Counter thought: I don't need to masturbate. I can control my urges and want to wait until I am with my wife to celebrate our marriage.

Stop, Drop, and Roll: Discovering and Correcting Dysfunctional Thoughts

Living in a sex-saturated society, it is important for members of the faith community to take time to assess and evaluate their thoughts regarding sex and sexual relationships. Especially for those whose lives have been affected by pornography and cybersex, there must be an effort to identify potentially unhealthy, dysfunctional thoughts, beliefs, assumptions, or expectations.

STOP
and identify thoughts, beliefs, assumptions, and expectations.

With your spouse or accountability partner, take time to brainstorm your thoughts regarding your sexual relationship and pornography. It is important to recognize that during this first step you don't get hung up on critical evaluation of the validity or veracity of your thoughts. This is brainstorming, not analysis. There are no "wrong" answers at this step. Later, of course, you may discover erroneous thoughts and choose to focus on an alternative interpretation. For now, focus your energy on articulating your thoughts, regardless of the degree of accuracy.

The purpose of this step is to reveal the minimizations, justifications, and "musterbations" that contribute to decisions to use pornography. To begin this process, couples are encouraged to ask themselves the following questions:

1. How frequently would you want to engage in sexual intimacy with your partner?

2. What are your expectations regarding initiation of sexual intimacy? Who should do what and when?

3. Consider five things about yourself that you might change (in regard to sexual intimacy) with your partner. Identify those statements that include the words "must" or "should."

4. Consider five things about your partner that you might change (in regard to sexual intimacy). Identify those statements that include the words "must" or "should."

5. How has the use of pornography benefited or helped you?

6. How has the use of pornography benefited your partner?

7. Has pornography helped you to better understand the needs/desires of the opposite sex? What have you learned?

8. If you have used Internet pornography, identify the excuses/explanations you have used to justify the behavior.

9. Have there been any fantasies that have emerged since you began using Internet pornography?

10. If you could choreograph a "perfect" sexual experience with your partner, what would be involved? Who would do what? Are any of your ideas associated with what you may have viewed in pornography?

DROP
the erroneous or
dysfunctional thoughts.

For each of the responses to the ten items in step one, you and your partner need to collaboratively decide the degree to which the thought, belief, or expectation is healthy or reasonable. For each item, identify those thoughts/attitudes/expectations that may have been shaped by an experience with pornography. Recognize those items that may be reflections of minimization, justification, or "musterbations."

It is very difficult for most people to effectively evaluate whether their thoughts, beliefs, or expectations are dysfunctional and that is why it is so important to continue this exercise with your spouse or professional counselor. The intention, of course, is to sort out healthy thoughts from those that may cause damage to the relationship. It is imperative that couples approach this step by engaging the basic listening skills described in chapter three. It would be suggested that this step be entered into prayerfully. Challenge yourself to avoid defensiveness.

ROLL
these thoughts into something
more healthy and productive.

You need to identify an alternative interpretation. For example, if a husband's use of pornography has led him to the belief that most women "want" sex more than his wife does, his thought process is distorted by the thought that "my wife never wants to have sex." A healthier, alternative thought would be "My wife seems to be more interested in sex when…"

The challenge, therefore, is to transform dysfunctional cognitions into healthier, alternative thoughts that honor both the relationship and God.

Covenant Reminder

In the book of Genesis, there is the description of God's covenant relationship with Abraham. In setting himself and his descendents apart from others whose religions and beliefs were centered on sexual excesses and the worship of fertility gods, Abraham agreed to a procedure in which the foreskin of the penis is removed. It is the mark of the covenant, a powerful symbol of being in relationship with God.

Although circumcision is not a requirement for membership within the Christian community, it continues to be an option that many parents elect for their infant sons. The issue is one of hygiene and aesthetics. Nonetheless, for Christian men who have been circumcised: be reminded of your covenant relationship with God. Whether standing at a urinal, making love to your wife, or being tempted to masturbate, be reminded that your behavior is to be reflective of that covenant relationship.

6

Lost in the Wilderness

The Dangerous Terrain of Internet Chatrooms

MARY'S STORY

I am the mother of three wonderful children, and a wife to a husband who works very hard to provide for our family. This is my second marriage. My first marriage lasted about five years. We married young, were both immature, and we found our lives going in different directions. He wanted the fast life filled with material things and fun, and I wanted to settle down and have children. We quickly grew apart and divorced. My family found it difficult to accept the divorce, but that is partially my fault. I had given them the clear impression that things were fine. I was too embarrassed to openly admit my marriage was falling apart.

A few years later I met Donald. He seemed like Mr. Right; an answer to prayer. My family loved and adored him and saw that I was beginning to feel happy again. We started our family, went from an apartment to a house, and life seemed to be going along quite well. We both agreed I would be a stay-at-home mother. There were some financial sacrifices, but it was worth it. I felt I could give my children everything they needed, and I loved being a mother.

My story really begins when my youngest daughter started kindergarten. The home seemed so quiet and empty. Yes, it provided some private time for myself, but it seemed like my kids were just growing up way to fast and I could sense they didn't need me as much as when they were younger. There was loneliness, some guilt over feeling bad because I had the "perfect" life, and a sense I was growing older. I started working out because I had been putting on some weight, but exercise has never been something I looked forward to, so it didn't last very long. I wasn't too pleased with what I saw in the mirror, so I got a makeover, changing the color and length of my hair. I spent way too much money on new clothes. But still, none of it made me feel any better.

So here I was, unhappy with myself, feeling older, feeling like my kids didn't need me as much, and wondering where my life was headed.

And my marriage? This is hard to explain and talk about, but things seemed to have changed over time. He was busy with work, putting in lots of hours. We seemed to be growing apart, gradually and slowly over time. The excitement that we once had faded away. We had drifted apart. I felt he was losing interest in me. I felt lonely, old, and unattractive.

It was out of boredom that I started using the Internet. It wasn't like I was looking for pornography or anything distasteful like that. I'm not sure what I was looking for, but I can tell you that what I found almost ruined my life.

When I first went exploring online, I had no clue as to what danger awaited me. I was rather innocent and naive about the computer, and especially the Internet. But once I figured out how to click a few buttons, I started writing letters to family and friends, and once in awhile, I actually talked to my girlfriend online using something called instant messaging. You just make up a screen name, give it to your friend, put your friend's name on something called a buddy list, and then start chatting when you see them online. It was so easy, and so fun. It really helped pass the time, and gave me something to do. I felt I had graduated to the modern era of technology.

Well, this is where my life's journey takes a sad turn. Actually, this is very embarrassing to talk about, but I'm determined to tell my story and deal with my guilt and shame. By telling my story I hope that other women can avoid the same mistakes I've made.

I remember that one fall day where the leaves had turned colors and it seemed rather dark and gloomy. The kind of day when you just want to stay home, drink some coffee, and curl up with a good book. I was bored, somewhat lonely, and was tired of all the housework. So, I went online.

I wrote a few emails to friends, and then just out of curiosity I checked out the chatrooms listed by our Internet provider. There were so many chatrooms with different titles and themes, and it was amazing. Some rooms are created by the Internet provider (we used America Online), but many rooms are made up by other people who use the same Internet company.

I started exploring. The first chatroom I went into was one called "gardening." People were just talking about gardening, and everyone seemed friendly. I didn't say a word, and just watched the conversation unfold. When I say, "talking," it just means people were typing their thoughts, and you can see what you and others type on the computer screen. When you enter a chatroom, sometimes people say "hello" or "welcome" to the room. It is entirely up to you if you want to respond back in some way.

Although "chatting" with people I couldn't see or know seemed awkward at first, I gradually became more comfortable and it didn't seem so odd anymore. I could talk with people in the privacy of my own home and it was so anonymous. No one could actually see me or hear my voice. And, it was sort of fun. Some people actually formed online friendships and would chat with each other whenever they were both online. The "regulars" in the garden chatroom seemed to know that I was a "newbie," which means I was a new person to the chatroom.

Over a period of weeks, I started exploring different kinds of chatrooms. Many of the chatroom names were overtly sexual and offensively explicit and I was careful to stay away from them. I didn't even want to imagine what was going on in those rooms and it didn't appeal to me one bit. Instead, I went to a chatroom called "married and flirting." I was curious as to what went on there.

As soon as I entered the room, people I didn't even know where trying to strike up a conversation with me in the room or sending me one of those private instant messages. They were all men vying for my attention. Some introduced themselves by saying something quite sexual, while others were more polite. Men right away wanted to know my age, what I looked like, where I lived, and if I was happily married. It felt like guys were swarming all over me, and frankly I liked the attention.

It became a matter of routine, after a while, that I would visit the "married and flirting" chatroom. Part of the experience, I admit, was rather distasteful. I'll never forget this one guy who would send me an instant message every time I signed on the computer. It was so annoying. He was relentless in asking for my personal picture and suggesting we meet offline for some conversation and fun. It always amazed me how fast some people wanted to chat over the phone and even meet in person when they didn't really even know me. I mean, how do you know these guys aren't some stalkers, or worse yet, rapists? After all, they talked so graphically about sexual stuff. It was gross!

Some guys even sent pictures of themselves over the computer. Once in awhile I would open the email to see what they looked like. Some sent naked pictures of themselves, and frankly I thought that was kind of gross. How could someone send a naked picture of themselves to someone they didn't even know? But the guys I chatted with assured me many women send pictures like that, chat on the phone, and even meet in person. Maybe so, but that seemed so dangerous to me, and sleazy. I wasn't that type of girl. Or was I?

Well, one day, I chatted with this man online who actually seemed very nice. I wasn't sure at first if he was genuine or if it was just a game to try to win over my trust. He was married, had several children, and openly admitted he was bored in his marriage. Apparently, the intimacy in his marriage had been lacking for some time. We seemed to hit it off quite well. He never pressured me for pictures or phone calls, so my comfort level with him grew over time. It's funny how sometimes you can tell personal things about your life to people you've never met. Maybe it has to do with the whole thing being anonymous. In any case, we developed an online friendship.

Part of me felt guilty talking to a man I didn't really know, but the more we chatted the more I felt I knew him. The more we chatted, the more I started believing that he knew me better than my own husband. The more we chatted, the more I started to think I was falling in love.

Looking back, we were both needy for some attention and affection. He seemed like a good listener so I shared some of my frustrations about my marriage with him. We were developing what I've come to learn is an online emotional affair. Who me? An online emotional affair? It's embarrassing to admit to. But, yes, emotional online affairs do occur, and I'm living proof of how easily it can happen.

One day, he suggested that we had reached the point in our relationship where we should meet. I was very conflicted about this suggestion and scared too. But there was a part of me that wanted to see and hear from the person I had been sharing personal stories with. Initially, I said no. But over the next few months my husband and I were having more and more disagreements and I felt myself growing more distant from him. Having met someone online with whom I could talk so freely, why couldn't I have something similar with my husband? I began to tell myself that perhaps God wanted me to have a closer, more meaningful relationship with someone else.

Six months after our initial encounter in the chatroom, plans were made to meet my new friend.

Not wanting to be seen, we arranged to meet at a restaurant about an hour away from my home. As I drove, I felt a hint of guilt knowing that I was taking a step away from my marriage. But the guilt was superceded by a desire to be emotionally close with someone. I was lonely and wanted desperately to be loved and cherished. I felt I deserved better in life.

As I approached to restaurant, I could feel the anticipation well up within me. I stopped at a traffic light and strained my eyes, wondering if I could catch a glimpse of the one who would rescue me from my dull existence. But my eye caught something else. Across the street from the restaurant: a church steeple atop of which was a cross.

I didn't notice the light turn green, nor did I hear the guy behind me honk his horn. The driver in that car actually had gotten out of his vehicle and tapped on my car window. I was in tears. Sobbing. He asked if I was all right and I assured him I was. But it was a lie. Something was terribly wrong. And if I had not seen that cross, it could have been a whole lot worse.

I turned the car around to head home, crying most of the way. I needed to talk to someone, but who is there that could understand what was going through my head and heart?

I drove straight to our church, hoping to talk to the pastor, but he was out of the office visiting some people at the hospital. And so I waited.

I waited in the sanctuary, trying to pull myself together.

And I prayed.

Lost in the Wilderness: Chatrooms for the Lonely

The Internet, and specifically its array of chatrooms, is like a wilderness. It may be interesting to explore, but there is darkness lurking everywhere to those unaware of the dangerous traps that lie ahead. For many, the Internet is a curious place, and seems harmless. But for women like Mary, her curiosity led her astray.

Mary was married, but she was also lonely. There was a void in her life. She did not understand this void and sometimes felt depressed. Her experience was difficult for her to talk about. Many find it challenging to talk about their marriages and admit they are lonely or needy. Many feel guilty, believing they should be content with life's circumstances, and don't want to come across as complainers or ungrateful. Some feel their partners are insensitive, and over time the joy and the glow of the wedding day has faded. Mary kept her feelings to herself. She felt lonely, but had difficulty understanding why she had these feelings. Mary's loneliness made her vulnerable in the wilderness.

There are many men online waiting for women like Mary to appear. They search the Internet, cruising chatrooms, trying to start up conversations. Some are very bold and demanding of sexual chat. This is turnoff for many women. However, there are some men more clever in their approach who say the right things to make the lonely women feel important. When one is needy and lonely, hearing compliments from someone they don't even know can feel good. It may seem odd or silly to some, but some people are attracted to this type of interaction. In a misleading way, the anonymity of the virtual interaction causes a person to feel safe. Identities are cloaked on the Internet, and the environment of chatrooms provides a place for people to interact with no measure of commitment.

Some men are very manipulative and deceptive, telling the women what ever she wants to hear. They can be good listeners, and come across as caring. For someone like Mary, this made her feel good. The more one travels to the wilderness, the risk of losing a perspective on how the Internet is affecting one gets clouded and distorted. We all have needs, emotional and physical, and if these needs are not being met in a relationship like a marriage, the temptation to stray becomes stronger, especially over the Internet.

There are some men who are lonely just like Mary. There are chatrooms set up with titles such as "Bored and Married," "Married and Flirting," "Hot Christian Wives," "Talk With A Pastor," "Listening Friend," and "Affairs and Cheating." Some lonely married men are seeking companionship too, and just like Mary, people can find each other and become emotionally attracted to one another. Loneliness makes us feel bad. It's a difficult feeling to have for any long period of time. It can make us feel sad and depressed, unworthy and unloved. It's a very powerful emotion.

Mary's judgment changed over time. She was vulnerable. She began to fill this need on the Internet. She knew what she was doing was wrong, but over time, she let her guard down more and more. She took more risks, justifying or rationalizing her behavior along the way. The Internet is a very seductive place. Ones feelings can get hurt, and voids superficially filled. When Mary found her way out of the wilderness, she had to deal with a lot of guilt and shame. She put herself and marriage at risk. Fortunately, she found the light, and the light guided her out of darkness.

Scriptural Guidance
for Those Lost in the Wilderness

The desert and the parched land will be glad;
*   The wilderness will rejoice and blossom.*
Like the crocus, it will burst into bloom;
*   It will rejoice greatly and shout for joy.*
The glory of Lebanon will be given to it,
*   The splendor of Carmel and Sharon;*
They will see the glory of the Lord,
*   The splendor of our God.*

And a highway will be there;
*   It will be called the Way of Holiness.*
The unclean will not journey on it;
*   It will be for those who walk in that Way;*
*   Wicked fools will not go about on it.*
No lion will be there,

> *Nor will any ferocious beast get up on it;*
> *They will not be found there.*
> *But only the redeemed will walk there.*
> *And the ransomed of the Lord will return.*
> *They will enter Zion with singing;*
> *Everlasting joy will crown their heads.*
> *Gladness and you will overtake them,*
> *And sorrow and sighing will fell away.*

ISA. 35:1–2, 8–10, NIV

> *Comfort, comfort my people, says your God.*
> *Speak tenderly to Jerusalem, and proclaim to her*
> *That her hard service has been completed,*
> *That her sin has been paid for,*
> *That she has received from the Lord's hand*
> *Double for all her sins.*

> *A voice of one calling:*
> *In the desert prepare the way for the Lord;*
> *Make straight in the wilderness*
> *A highway for our God.*
> *Every valley shall be raised up,*
> *Every mountain and hill made low;*
> *The rough ground shall become level,*
> *The rugged places a plain.*
> *And the glory of the Lord will be revealed,*
> *And all mankind together will see it.*
> *For the mouth of the Lord has spoken.*

ISA. 40:1–5, NIV

Have you ever been hiking and gotten lost? It's easy to get lost in a wilderness. The size and sameness of mile after mile is disorienting and discomforting. You climb hill after hill hoping that each one will provide a newer perspective, one that will reveal the way home. Yet each hilltop provides the same view as the one before. You begin to think that you are so lost that you will never find your way out again. You feel totally alone and vulnerable and frightened.

The Hebrew people knew the wilderness experience. After Moses led them in Exodus out of bondage in Egypt they wandered in wilderness for forty years. So when Old Testament authors speak of the wilderness, they evoke the memory of a time of lonesome wandering in a barren land; a time when the Hebrew people felt alone and forsaken by God.

A wilderness can be a physical reality, such as the wilderness in which the Hebrews wandered for forty years or Jesus' wilderness experience after his baptism. But the wilderness is more than a physical place. In the Bible, the wilderness is also a metaphor for times when we feel lost and lonely. The wilderness is a metaphor for times we find ourselves in danger or trouble. It is a symbol of times when we feel distant from God. The wilderness is a metaphor for the paths we take in our life's journey when we venture into dangerous terrain and discover how lost we have become. At times like that, we cry out to God, praying to Creator, Redeemer, Sustainer to rescue us.

These passages from the Book of Isaiah speak of a time when the Hebrew people were feeling lost. It was during the time of the Babylonian exile. In 587 B.C., the Babylonians had invaded the city of Jerusalem and destroyed the Temple of Solomon. Many of the Hebrew people were forced into exile, living in the barren, arid land of Babylon. It was as if they were again wandering in the wilderness.

In chapter thirty-five, the prophet Isaiah describes what would happen if God would appear in the wilderness. The dry and barren land will burst forth in bloom; then waters will rush out to fill streams and pools, and green grasses will grow. The wilderness will be transformed. And in the midst of its vast desolation a road will be built; a highway so broad and wide that shows the people of God the way back home to Jerusalem. And this highway will be visible from everywhere and so easy to travel on that no one would again get lost in the wilderness.

That highway will save the people of God from forever wandering hopelessly in the wilderness. They will travel on God's highway and they will know who they are and where they are to go. And they will know that this is God's highway, according to the prophet Isaiah in chapter thirty-five because those who are blind will be able to see, those who are deaf will be able to hear, those who are lame will leap like deer, and those who could not speak will sing for joy.

Jesus Christ is God's highway, God's presence in the wilderness.

Those whose lives have been affected by pornography and cybersex find themselves in wilderness. At the beginning of this chapter you read about Mary who found herself going down a dangerous path as she explored the world of cyber-sexual chatrooms. Others like her find themselves lost in the wilderness terrain of cybersex and Internet pornography. Like spending time in a real wilderness, their wilderness can leave them feeling lonely and hopelessly lost. By their own actions they have distanced themselves from marriage partners, family, and God. When they realize the mistakes they've made; when they realize how lost they have become, they look for a way out, a path, something that will show them where to go, how to get out of the wilderness.

The way out is found in Jesus Christ.

Strategies for Finding Your Way out of the Wilderness

Experts in the field of remote wilderness exploration will tell you that if you ever get lost, the key to survival is to stay calm. Those who panic tend to take action before thinking, and their chances for survival can be jeopardized. When lost, it is essential to relax and focus attention. Your chances for survival increase exponentially if you follow three primary survival strategies: First, get your bearings. Second, move in a constant direction (preferably using a compass). And, third, constantly scan the horizon for signs of potential rescue.

The Prayer of the Prodigal

When experiencing significant shame, many Christians find it difficult to pray, not knowing what words to use. After all, how does one approach God in the aftermath of sexual sin?

Like the prodigal son, the first step is to go home to be greeted by a forgiving father. It will be a humbling experience and your hesitancy may be in the scarcity of words and language to describe your emotions. It is suggested, therefore, that in your prayers you do the following:

Center your thoughts on the majesty of God. This is the great Creator, the maker of the heavens and the earth. This is your creator who formed you in your mother's womb. Center your thoughts also on God's son, Jesus Christ. By his birth, death, and resurrection, your sins have been forgiven. By his sacrifice you have the privilege to return to relationship with God. Center your thoughts as well on the Holy Spirit who has guided you to discover the error of your ways, inviting you to return to God. By centering your thoughts on God the Creator, Redeemer, and Sustainer, your will find the language to appropriately praise and celebrate your Lord. And in so doing, you will sense God embracing you, just as the prodigal's father greeted his wayward child.

Get Your Bearings

Having wandered into the dangerous terrain of Internet chat-rooms, Mary soon discovered the trouble she was getting herself into. Finding the way out of the mess she had created first required her to assess her situation. She knew she had made a mistake, that's for sure.

Make your confession. God already knows what you have done, so this is not an exercise in informing God of your actions. This is an opportunity for you to conduct a full inventory of your sin. Focus on the effect your behavior has had on your relationship with God, with others, and its effect on you. Consider the manner in which you should have conducted yourself and recognize how far from that standard you were.

Celebrate forgiveness. Whether tears of gratitude or joyful smile, allow God's Spirit to wash you clean of your sin. Unlike times before, however, when you offered glib and cursory confession, your current action is a pledge, a commitment to a different way of life. No longer will you offer prayers only in times of crisis or fleeting moments of remorse. Now you will celebrate your renewed relationship with God through a spiritual discipline of daily prayer.

Ask for divine guidance. Again, this is a time for you to consider what you need in order to stay committed to this renewed relationship with God, marriage partner, and family. Consider those factors that put you at risk of relapse. Give thought to circumstances that may compromise your sexual or moral sobriety. Do not leave it to God to magically protect you. In prayer, allow God's Spirit to help you devise and plan specific strategies to guard and protect you.

The primary means by which she was able to stay calm was prayer.

Her story is a marvelous example of an individual who upon recognizing her dilemma, turned immediately to God in prayer. It gave her focus. It allowed her to center and concentrate her focus on her redeemer. It allowed her an opportunity to make an accurate assessment of who she is and what she had done.

Mary prayed to strengthen her relationship with God and husband. Prayer and spiritual devotion helped her resist any future temptations to reconnect with the Internet and search out relationships on those days she felt down and discouraged. Through prayer she came to realize that the Internet was no longer an option for coping with loneliness. Sometimes people are tempted in their area of weakness or vulnerability. It's best to recognize that temptation to relapse will likely occur, but knowing this in itself provides strength to resist the temptation because one will less likely be caught off guard.

Move in a Constant Direction

If lost in the woods or wilderness, rescue can be dependent on whether you are walking in circles or proceeding in one constant direction. Whether it is north, south, east, or west, chose one direction and stay in that direction. Whether following the sun that rises in the east and sets in the west, or if your direction is guided by moss growing on the north side of trees, or whether you look toward the heavens to be guided by the North Star, your survival may depend on traveling in one set direction. And, of course, if you have a compass, use it!

When lost in the wilderness of cybersex and Internet pornography, set your spiritual direction to move constantly toward God. Avoid paths that may divert or distract you from returning to that relationship. Scripture serves as a compass to keep you on that path. It is suggested you design a schedule of regular Bible reading, doing so especially when in times past you strayed into using the computer for selfish reasons. At times of greatest weakness, God's Word will help keep you in the path toward redemption.

Continually Scan the Horizon

Persons who are trying to find their way when lost in the wilderness intuitively know to watch the horizon for signs of civilization. Especially in the dark of night, lights in the distance are a heartening discovery because it indicates that shelter and aid will soon be available.

Scanning the horizon means looking for community. It means actively searching for resources to assist you.

In relationships and marriages where one or both struggle with some aspect of the relationship, its acceptable and often wise to seek out counsel from other Christians. This can include seeking pastoral guidance, or professional counseling. Some times people are embarrassed to go to counseling, but don't let pride get in the way. Counselors are trained to help people who are stuck. They can shed light on the problems and offer solutions. Most clinicians are sensitive and realize clients are embarrassed to discuss their problems in such a setting, and you can be certain that an effort will be made to help you feel more comfortable.

Mary needed to repair the trust and bond with her husband. She needed to communicate her loneliness and needs for affection that were going unmet. She and her husband needed to talk openly about their marriage. Sometimes when couples struggle with this type of communication, or anger and tension is so strong that it feels unsafe to express oneself openly, a counselor can help couples break this impasse.

7

My Deep Dark Secret

The Destructive Cycle of Sexual Abuse

JEFF'S STORY

Sitting on the edge of the bed, I put a single bullet into the chamber of my father's revolver. I spun the chamber and listened to each click for what felt like an eternity, until if finally stopped. With my eyes tightly closed, I raised and pressed the barrel of the gun against my temple. I cried out in despair, "Lord, let me live or let me die. My fate is in your hands." Click! The silence was deafening.

■ ■ ■

So how did my life reach a point of such despair that I tried to kill myself on more than one occasion?

My story begins several years ago when I was a child. When I was in the fourth grade, I was sexually abused by a male babysitter for over a year. About once a month, my parents would go out for a night on the town. Gary was the son of my parents' best friends. They had been friends and neighbors for many years, and Gary was like a trusted member of our family. We went to the same church, and Gary was a Boy Scout. I liked Gary and always had fun when he babysat me. My parents had no reason to mistrust him; he was always friendly and polite and joked around in a fun way.

One night, Gary introduced to me to a game he called "truth or dare." He started the game by asking me to do silly things like jump up and down or make animal sounds. It was funny and we laughed a lot. We played this game every time he babysat me. One night, the game changed. We started out acting silly just like before, but as the game went on Gary dared me to touch his private parts. He told me touching his private parts was all part of the game and it would be a lot of fun. He took his penis out from under his shorts and told me to rub it for him. He told me to move my hand up and down, and he even showed me how to do it by putting his hand on top of mine. I did what he wanted me to because I was confused and too afraid to tell him no. He said I did a good job and I was winning the game. After a few minutes, Gary said the game was over. He removed my hand and put his penis back in his shorts.

Gary told me I should never tell anyone about this game because our parents would get mad and I'd get in trouble. This seemed con-fusing to me because I thought it was just a game, but since I didn't want to get in trouble or make Gary mad at me, I didn't tell anyone about the game. It was our little secret.

Over time, Gary's truth and dare game evolved and included much more touching than the first time we played. I touched his penis and he touched mine. It felt good when he touched mine. It sort of tickled. He told me the tickling feeling was good. He'd always tell me afterwards that the game was our secret and I'd get in trouble if I told. He also told me he'd be really mad at me if I told our secret and wouldn't play with me anymore. He said his parents would be so mad, I wouldn't be allowed to go swimming in their swimming pool, and so I kept my promise. The secret was safe with me.

As Gary's game evolved over the course of a year, my feelings about the game changed. It wasn't fun anymore. I felt like something was wrong, but I wasn't sure what to do about it and I didn't want to get in trouble. It seemed all Gary wanted to do when he babysat me was play that stupid game. Gary was sexually abusing me, but I didn't know that then. It was rather traumatic to me; I'll skip the grizzly details. It's still unpleasant to talk about it to this day. I never told my parents of the abuse until I got in trouble with the law. I'll talk more about that later.

■ ■ ■

The secret I kept about my abuse burned inside of me for a very long time, but like many victims of abuse I was too ashamed and embarrassed to talk openly about it. I was also a little afraid of Gary. He told me never to tell of our game, and since he was older than me, I listened. I also thought that if I kept it secret, then the bad feelings I had about the abuse and myself would somehow go away over time.

Gary and his family eventually moved away, so the abuse stopped. I missed Gary, but I was glad we didn't have to play the game anymore. I tried to forget about it, but I couldn't get it out of my head. I wanted to tell someone, but I was still afraid Gary would find out and we would get in trouble just like he warned.

To this day, I'm still not totally sure why I didn't tell my parents when I suspected something was wrong. I think they would've believed me, but something inside kept me from telling the secret. Maybe I really believed my parents would be mad and blame me for what happened. I also didn't want to lose Gary's friendship or not be able to swim in his pool. For a long time I believed I'd done something wrong and shouldn't have let Gary touch me. I felt I was to blame for not making him stop.

During my teenage years, I struggled with many issues that I now believe are directly connected to my abuse. I was often depressed, but put on this mask and tried to act like everything was OK. I had some friends, but it was hard to let anyone get close to me. I was afraid they would somehow find out about the abuse and stop liking me.

I tried hard not to think about it, but this became more difficult when I reached puberty. I liked girls, but there was a part of me that secretly worried I might be gay. I didn't have sexual feelings for guys so I told myself I mustn't be. But in the back of my mind, I always worried about it. I worried that if my peers found out I had been abused by a guy, they would think I was gay. I wanted to be invisible. I've learned this is a common worry for boys who've been abused by males. I felt so alone. I wondered what was wrong with me, but there was no way I was going to openly talk about this with anyone. I worried if I opened up just a little, someone would be able to figure out I'd been abused.

As I became more depressed, I felt like staying home more than going out with friends. I didn't go to football or basketball games like other kids my age. Home felt much safer than the social world of school. I was tired a lot, sometimes sad without knowing why, and my social confidence was in the pits. I knew I was missing out on life, but I really didn't care. The more socially isolated I became, the more depressed I felt. It was a very vicious cycle that I didn't know how to break.

The only friends I had at the time were two cousins, who introduced me to video games. I quickly became hooked on them because I could play by myself and safely retreat from the real world. Before long, I told my parents I needed a computer for school. I think they agreed because they hoped it would make me happy.

I quickly learned the ins and outs of computers, including the Internet. One day while working on a homework assignment, I went to a Web site I thought would be appropriate for the topic I was researching. To my amazement, pictures of hot-looking naked women popped up! I was excited by what I saw. I followed the link for a free tour of the site. Wow, more pictures!

I became addicted to pornography overnight. I never spent any money on buying porno pictures and I didn't need to—they were all free. I became so obsessed over time that I would keep my computer running all day downloading as many pictures as I could. I collected thousands of images every day, far too many to ever look at. So I'd save them onto discs.

Most nights I'd look at the pictures and masturbate. It made me feel good, at least temporarily. Sometimes I'd sit at the computer for hours, getting aroused, but holding off my orgasm until I found just the right picture that pushed me over the excitement edge. It was like I was in a trance, losing all perspective of time.

I kept my door locked so my parents wouldn't walk in on me. Sometimes they'd ask what I was doing all night in my room with the door locked. I'd just lie. I said I was doing a school project and needed privacy. They had no clue what I was really up to. If by chance they would walk in on me, I knew how to change the computer screen really fast and hide the pornography. I'd sometimes get mad at them and even yell at them if they interrupted me. It was like they were spoiling my private time.

I continued to go to school but didn't have many friends. My grades really suffered, and I lost interest in school altogether. Most of the time I daydreamed about the pornography I'd be viewing when I got home.

I thought about my sexual abuse often, but still kept it secret. My self-esteem was so low. I felt trapped. There were times I thought about suicide. [Add more here about the attempts mentioned in the beginning?] I thought about hanging myself or shooting myself. The depth of my pain was too much to bear most of the time. Even though masturbation and pornography gave me some temporary relief, the problems were always there. It's like the more depressed and isolated I became, the more I escaped to my computer. I could control the computer. I couldn't control people.

One day while online, my cousin instant-messaged me. He suggested I contact this girl he'd met online. (I'll refer to her as Shayla, even though that's not her real name.) I sent her an instant message, and she responded right away. It was so cool. We chatted for a little bit, nothing too serious. Over the next few weeks, we struck up a friendship and shared more about ourselves.

Shayla lived with her parents, who argued and fought a lot, and she was very unhappy and depressed, just like me. I also found out that she was younger than me, a minor, in fact. But I didn't dwell on that too much. A girl was talking to me, taking interest in me even! Who cared how old she was?

She even shared with me that she'd been abused. I felt reassured that there was someone out there like me, someone who could relate to me.

I finally got up the courage and told her I'd been sexually abused when I was younger, and she was very understanding. She didn't make fun of me or reject me. She just had a way about her that made me feel truly understood.

I noticed my feelings for Shayla starting to grow. I had another reason for looking forward to coming home from school now. I hoped she'd be online so we could chat, but I never told her about my pornography problem. I didn't want to risk scaring her away. It's funny how I could tell her about my abuse, but not about my pornography problem. Maybe I didn't even realize how serious my problem was at the time I met her. But collecting porn pictures had become as much a part of my daily life as brushing my teeth. I didn't want to reveal that part of myself. I guess I was still keeping secrets.

One day Shayla suggested we send each other pictures of ourselves. I was excited about seeing what she looked like, yet nervous that she would think I was ugly and reject me. Plus, I knew in the back of my mind she was a minor. I was so needy for a friend; I didn't want her age to matter.

We each had digital cameras, so we took pictures and sent them to each another. She was so cute, I couldn't believe it. The next day, however, she wasn't online. My worst fear was confirmed: she thought I was ugly and didn't want to chat anymore. I was instantly depressed again, and felt sick to my stomach. I told my parents I had the flu and stayed home from school the next day.

I did nothing but lie around, feeling depressed. Later in the day, when I knew she was home from school, I got on the computer to see if she was online. She was. I wanted to send her an instant message, but I was afraid she would ignore me. I sat there, just staring at the computer screen. And then, she sent me a message. A friendly message. She apologized for not being online the previous day. We started to chat again. I was euphoric. She still liked me.

As time when on, I suggested we send naked pictures of ourselves to each other. To my delightful surprise, Shayla agreed. That was such a rush. I started to think of her as my girlfriend. Even though I didn't really know her, I thought I did, and her sending pictures to me made me feel she really cared for me. Sometimes, I masturbated to her naked pictures. I never told her that. But doing so made me feel closer to her.

One day, she suggested we talk on the phone and even meet each other. She lived in another state, so meeting didn't seem that practical, but I called her. Her voice was so cute. I was falling in love. Finally, a girl who liked me! I didn't care that she was a lot younger. She made me feel good about myself. That's all that mattered.

We arranged to meet. I was going to skip school, borrow my parents' car, and drive the three hours to meet her. I couldn't sleep the entire week. Thoughts of Shayla and the sex we might have consumed me.

As I was driving to meet her, though, I was tempted to turn around and go home. A voice in my head kept telling me this was wrong and I could get in trouble. But it was too late. I had to meet her and see who the girl of my dreams was, in person.

We'd planned to meet in a hotel room in a not-so-good part of town. I got lost a few times, but finally found the hotel. After parking the car, I took a deep breath and knocked on the door. The door opened, and to my surprise, I was tackled by three police officers who forced my hands behind my back and handcuffed them. They put me in a police car and drove me to jail. I was shaking all over and felt like I wanted to cry. It was the worst moment of my life.

I never did meet Shayla. I later learned she was scared of meeting me and told one of her girlfriends about our plans. Her girlfriend told her parents, who then called the police.

I was allowed to make one phone call from jail. That was the hardest phone call I ever made to my parents. I stuttered at first, but finally told my mother what happened. She cried a lot. I then told my dad. He was quiet. That meant he was too angry to say anything. I'd let both my parents down. I just wanted them to tell me everything would be OK. I felt so utterly alone.

The police were not supportive. In fact, I could tell they thought I was a bad person by the way they treated me and talked to me.

They thought I meant to harm Shayla, which was so not true. But they didn't believe me and made me feel like such a loser.

They fingerprinted me and took my picture. They told me I was being arrested. They advised me to call an attorney. Who would I call? I didn't know any attorneys. I had never gotten in trouble before. I didn't know what to do. I waited for my parents to come see me. That was longest wait of my life. I was put in a holding cell with some scary-looking men. They looked like hardened criminals.

After my parents posted bail, I was let out of jail and allowed to go home with them. The ride home was silent. I didn't really know what to say. I was ashamed and embarrassed. I just wanted to close my eyes and make it all go away. It didn't go away, though; it was just the beginning of a long and frightening ordeal.

My parents found an attorney for me. He explained how much trouble I could be in. I didn't really understand all the legal words he used, so I kept quiet. My parents did the talking for me. The first recommendation he made was to call up a counselor he had worked with and trusted. My parents called the counselor and set up the first session for me. I was so scared to go to counseling. As it turned out, this is the best advice I was ever given. It took time to trust my counselor, but when I did, I told him my life story.

What I learned from counseling was that the actions that got me into trouble with the law stemmed from my past sexual abuse. That doesn't excuse my behavior, but it helped me to understand why I did what I did. For years I'd tried to cover up the abuse and mask my feelings, but I paid a high price. It doesn't really seem fair I had to suffer so much. I lost perspective on reality. I used the computer to hide behind and create what I thought was a safe haven in the privacy of my bedroom. I've learned my emotional pain made me feel vulnerable, so I turned to the computer and pornography to escape reality. I created a fantasy world.

I saw and experienced the dark side of online pornography first hand. The use of pornography made me more depressed. It allowed me to maintain my denial about my own abuse. Then, when Shayla began showing an interest in me, I fantasized that she was my girl-friend—and we'd never even met before! But she filled the need I had for companionship. After I lost her, I was sad for a very long time.

I haven't talked with her since that fateful day of my arrest. I got rid of all my Internet pornography. Every last picture. I never want to go back to that darkness again.

Since then, I finished high school and completed college. I joined a young-adults Bible study. I still get depressed now and then, but I don't think about suicide anymore. I know it will take time to completely get over my depression. And, I haven't looked at any por-nography in a long time. I'm on my way to recovery. And, oh yes, I even found a girlfriend who's my age.

Now I tell anyone who's been a victim of childhood abuse that it's important to talk about it and understand how it can affect you. I also tell anyone who'll listen to stay away from online pornography. It nearly ruined my life. Thank God, I'm free.

The Impact of Child Sexual Abuse

The destructive cycle of child abuse is a real issue for many. Sexual abuse happens to both boys and girls of all ages. Some victims of child abuse tell a trusted adult right away. This is a good thing. It stops the abuse from continuing in most cases. It takes a lot of courage for a child to disclose the abuse. However, many children are so confused, frightened, and ashamed, they keep their abuse secret for years, sometimes a whole lifetime, while suffering in silence. Some offenders scare children into keeping the abuse a secret. They tell children they will go to jail if caught. Some tell the child no adult will believe them and they will get into a lot of trouble. Offenders often tell children their mother will be angry and the abuse will lead to divorce. Some offend-ers are very clever in making the child feel they actively desired the abuse, and the child feels so guilty, they hide the secret, even from trusted adults or peers. Whatever the reason, children often are conflicted about reporting the abuse. They know or have a sense that the abuse is wrong, but it's just too hard to tell.

Sexual abuse damages children's self-esteem and self-worth. They feel dirty, bad about themselves, and betrayed by a trusted adult. Sometimes children are abused by older children in their neighborhoods, a relative, or someone the family trusts, like a babysitter. Sometimes a victim has felt emotionally close to their offender, like a father figure. They are torn between reporting the abuse and possibly breaking up their family, and hurting the paternal figure's feelings. They take a protective role and actually take care of the offender's emotional needs. Regardless of the type of abuse or the relationship between victim and offender, the abuse can have long-term emotional effects. This can include struggling with trust and intimacy in adult relationships, even marriages. Some victims hate sex because physical intimacy in marriage triggers old feelings of abuse. It's difficult for many to enjoy the physical aspect of a marriage. They feel inhibited and have a hard time trusting their partner and letting go of the past. They fear sexual pleasure in their lives because it makes them feel guilty and ashamed. It can be like reliving the abuse all over again. On the other hand, some victims react quite differently. They develop a pattern of sexual promiscuity. They bring sex into relationships because they feel this is one way to get attention and affection. They are confused about true love and intimacy. Deep down inside, they want love and affection, but have learned to try to get it in the wrong way. They may have no conscious realization their sexual behavior is related to their past abuse. They repeat this pattern over and over again, jumping in and out of relationships and losing their sense of self-respect along the way.

Sexual abuse affects people in different ways. Jeff's history of childhood sexual abuse played a major role in the development of his addiction to pornography. Despite a loving family, he kept his dark secret for a very long time. This impacted his psychological development in a negative way. He was traumatized by the abuse. Sexual abuse affects people in different ways. Not all victims of abuse engage in self-destructive patterns like Jeff. Some victims of abuse manage to survive their ordeal without trauma such as depression and suicide. For many, however, the impact of abuse is devastating and life-changing.

Jeff became depressed and suicidal. He felt ashamed, fearful of his parents' reaction if he disclosed the truth, and fearful of the offender's reaction to breaking the silence. Jeff blamed himself for the abuse even though he was only a child and it wasn't his fault. He developed low self-esteem and confidence, feelings of insecurity and inadequacy as a male, as well as social anxiety. All these dynamics made him fragile and vulnerable to the use of pornography. The computer and the Internet became Jeff's refuge, a temporary way to escape his inner pain. The more he withdrew from healthy social relationships, the more he depended on the Internet.

When Jeff discovered pornography, he was immediately aroused and excited. One picture led to two pictures, and over time, a pattern developed where he became addicted to pornography. He felt ashamed of this behavior, but because he was so lonely most of the time, he began to justify his actions. This justification led to greater usage, and he found himself trapped in this dark world. The more time he spent trying to find some pleasure through sexual arousal, the more depressed he became. The more depressed he became, the more he withdrew from healthy relationships. His pornography usage escalated. It was a vicious cycle, one from which he could not escape.

When Jeff first talked to a girl online, even though she was a minor, he felt a sense of social connection he was not achieving at school or through other types of social activities. He became a loner. The computer provided a barrier of safety. He didn't have to worry about rejection due to physical appearance. He was talking to someone and she was actually talking back. Given his neediness, this type of interaction made him feel better. He began to look forward to talking with this girl every day. That's all he thought about while at school. He wanted to get home as fast as he could, check to see if she wrote any emails, and ended up chatting with her into the late hours of the night. His school-work suffered. He was tired a lot. He lied to his parents, stating he was up late working on school projects. Despite knowing this girl was a minor, he began to care for her. He was developing a "virtual" relationship. As she shared personal information, he believed she cared for him. He began to form a mental picture of her although he had never seen her. He became attracted to her.

In the back of Jeff's mind he knew she might not be the girl he of his dreams; but his need for social connection was so strong he tried to block this out of his mind. As his confidence in the relationship grew, exchanging pictures over the Internet fueled his desire for her. He began to obsess about her and dreamed of a future together. Once his fear of rejection subsided, more pictures were exchanged. This was a big moment for Jeff. She still liked him afterwards, and he cherished the pictures she sent him. He taped her picture to his computer monitor every time he talked with her.

Exchanging pictures led to the next step of wanting to hear her voice and chat on the phone. She gave Jeff her phone number and he called her. Once he was comfortable talking on the phone, the desire to meet and see each other was the next natural step in their relationship. The more the fantasized relationship developed, the less Jeff thought about her being a minor. His desire for affection and attention was stronger than the reality of any social or legal consequences. Once Jeff decided to meet her, he blocked out any fear related to consequence. It didn't seem to matter; he'd found someone with whom he could bond emotionally.

When Jeff was confronted and arrested by the police, he was scared to death. His fantasy world came crashing down. Jeff was a good young man who really meant no harm to this girl. From his childhood abuse to his addiction to pornography, his life was spiraling downward for a very long time. Getting caught was actually a blessing in disguise. One example of this was that Jeff had to go to counseling. This led to disclosing his abuse to his parents, confronting his offender face to face, and eventually developing social confidence and esteem.

The healing process takes time. Jeff has made great strides in his personal growth. He has broken the bonds of pornography addiction and completed college, found a job, and developed a steady relationship with a girlfriend his age. Even though his story has a sad side to it, it's also a story about hope and renewal. One can overcome the impact of childhood sexual abuse. We see this every day in counseling. The road may be a challenging one, but many have the courage to cross the finish line. Fortunately, many resources exist to help this process.

Common Effects of Untreated Sexual Abuse

Sexual abuse affects victims in different ways. Some victims recover more rapidly than others and go on to live healthy and productive lives. For others, however, untreated symptoms of abuse persist into adulthood. According to The National Center for Post Traumatic Stress Disorders[1], victims of abuse frequently experience the following problems:

- Post-traumatic stress disorder or anxiety
- Depression and thoughts of suicide
- Sexual anxiety and disorders
- Poor body image and low self-esteem
- Unhealthy behaviors, such as alcohol abuse, drug abuse, self-mutilation, or binging and purging

Warning Signs of Child Sexual Abuse

The world has become an increasingly dangerous place for our children. We want to protect and keep them safe. No parent likes to think about sexual abuse. However, abuse is a real issue, and arming yourself with knowledge about the common warning signs of sexual abuse can help you keep them safe.

The Safe Child Program[2] defines sexual abuse as:

"… any sexual contact with a child or the use of a child for the sexual pleasure of someone else. This may include exposing private parts to the child or asking the child to expose him or herself, fondling of the genitals or requests for the child to do so, oral sex or attempts to enter the vagina or anus with fingers,

Common Fears about Reporting the Abuse

There are many reasons why victims of sexual abuse keep it a secret. Some of the most common reasons shared by male and female victims during counseling are:

- It's my fault.
- I'll get into some type of trouble.
- No one will believe me.
- My mom will be mad when he (dad or step dad) leaves.
- I'm confused; I don't know what to do.
- I feel ashamed and guilty.
- The offender might go to jail, and I still care about him.
- He won't like me anymore.
- He said he'd hurt me or someone in my family if I tell.

objects or penis, although actual penetration is rarely achieved."

There are a number of warning signs that a child may have been sexually abused. These include:

Physical Indicators

- Difficulty walking or sitting
- Torn clothing
- Stained or bloody underwear
- Pain or itching in genital area
- Venereal disease, especially in preteens
- Pregnancy

- I don't want to have to tell this story to strangers over and over again.
- I'm scared.
- I didn't make it stop.
- I'm too depressed to talk about it.
- I don't want to think about it. I'm trying to block it out of my mind.
- Kids at school will find out.
- They will call me gay.
- I'm afraid I'll have to testify in court.
- My parents won't trust me to go anywhere on my own again.
- My friends might shun me, hate me, or spread rumors about me.

Behavioral Indicators

- Inappropriate displays of affection

- Discomfort with or rejection of typical family affection

- Sleep problems, including insomnia, nightmares, refusal to sleep alone, or suddenly insisting on a night light

- Regressive behaviors, including thumb-sucking, bed-wetting, infantile behaviors, or other signs of dependency

- Extreme clinginess or other signs of fearfulness

- An unwillingness to participate in or reluctance to change clothing for gym class

- Bizarre or unusual sophistication pertaining to sexual behavior or knowledge, including sexual acting out

- Reports of sexual assault by a parent or guardian

- Sudden changes in behavior or school performance

- Learning problems (or difficulty concentrating) that cannot be attributed to specific physical or psychological causes

- Watchfulness, as if preparing for something bad to happen

- Unusual compliance, passivity, or withdrawal

- A pattern of arriving early to activities, staying late, and not wanting to go home

- Noticeable fear of a particular person or certain places

- Unusual or unexpected response from the child when questioned about being touched by someone

- Unreasonable fear of a physical exam

- Drawings depicting sexual acts

- A sudden awareness of genitals and sexual acts and words
- Attempts to get other children to perform sexual acts

Statistics[3]

- 1 in 4 girls is sexually abused before the age of 18.
- 1 in 6 boys is sexually abused before the age of 18.
- 1 in 5 children are solicited sexually while on the internet.
- An estimated 39 million survivors of childhood sexual abuse exist in America today.
- 30-40% of victims are abused by a family member.
- Another 50% are abused by someone outside of the family whom they know and trust.
- Approximately 40% are abused by older or larger children whom they know.
- Only 10% of abuse victims are abused by strangers.
- The median age for reported abuse is 9 years old.
- More than 20% of children are sexually abused before the age of 8.
- Almost 80% initially deny abuse or are tentative in disclosing. Of those who do disclose, approximately 75% disclose accidentally. Additionally, of those who do disclose, more than 20% eventually recant even though the abuse occurred.
- Fabricated sexual abuse reports constitute only 1% to 4% of all reported cases. Of these reports, 75% are falsely reported by adults and 25% are reported by children. Children only fabricate ½% of the time.

Scriptural Guidance
for Those in the Depths of Despair

In the vignette that introduced this chapter, Jeff was so distraught with his circumstances that he seriously considered suicide. For Jeff and others who experience this depth of despair, these words from the Old Testament may be particularly helpful:

> Now Ahab told Jezebel everything Elijah had done and how he had killed all the prophets with the sword. So Jezebel sent a messenger to Elijah to say, "May the gods deal with me, be it ever so severely, if by this time tomorrow I do not make your life like that of one of them."
>
> Elijah was afraid and ran for his life. When he came to Beersheba in Judah, he left his servant there, while he himself went a day's journey into the desert. He came to a broom tree, sat down under it and prayed that he might die. "I have had enough, Lord," he said. "Take my life; I am no better than my ancestors." Then he lie down under the tree and fell asleep.
>
> All at once an angel touched him and said, "Get up and eat." He looked around, and there by his head was a cake of bread baked over hot coals and a jar of water. He ate and drank and then lay down again.
>
> The angel of the Lord came back a second time and touched him and said, "Get up and eat, for the journey is too much for you." So he got up and ate and drank. Strengthened by that food, he traveled forty days and forty nights until he reached Horeb, the mountain of God. There he went into a cave and spent the night.
>
> And the word of the Lord came to him: "What are you doing here, Elijah?"
>
> He replied, "I have been very zealous for the Lord God Almighty. The Israelites have rejected your covenant,

broken down your altars, and put your prophets to death with the sword. I am the only one left, and now they are trying to kill me too."

The Lord said, "Go out and stand on the mountain in the presence of the Lord, for the Lord is about to pass by."

Then a great and powerful wind tore the mountains apart and shattered the rocks before the Lord, but the Lord was not in the wind. After the wind there was an earthquake, but he Lord was not in the earthquake. After the earthquake there was a fire, but the Lord was not in the fire. And after the fire came a gentle whisper. When Elijah heard it, he pulled his cloak over his face and went out and stood in the mouth of the cave.

Then a voice said to him, "What are you doing here, Elijah?"

He replied, "I have been very zealous for the Lord God Almighty. The Israelites have rejected your covenant, broken down your altars, and put your prophets to death with the sword. I am the only one left, and now they are trying to kill me too."

The Lord said to him, "Go back the way you came, and go to the Desert of Damascus.

I KINGS 19:1–15, NIV

This story about Elijah is not just a Scripture passage that tells of bit of prophetic history. This is a story that tells us how to see the light of God when we are in our darkest moments. Elijah was someone who knew hopelessness; he knew what it is to face a river of despair. He was so low and dejected, perhaps depressed, that he prayed for his own death, saying, "I have had enough, Lord," "take my life...."

The day before Elijah was anything but depressed. The day before he was on Mt. Carmel demonstrating the power of

God by performing a miracle. But soon after he also ordered the slaughter of pagan "prophets of Baal."

These "prophets of Baal," though, belonged to Queen Jezebel, and when she found out what Elijah had done, she was enraged. And as it says in the beginning of this passage from I Kings, Queen Jezebel sent a messenger to Elijah to inform him that she wanted retribution and she had every intention of hunting him down to kill him.

Elijah ran for his life; he fled into the desert. But his desert land wasn't just a barren piece of land. Elijah's desert wilderness was emotional and spiritual as well. For it is there that he found himself sitting under a tree praying, "I have had enough, Lord, take away my life...."

As it says in the text, *"Then he lie down under the tree and fell asleep. All at once an angel touched him and said, "Get up and eat... He ate and drank and then lay down again."* In the midst of his wilderness experience, Elijah experienced the sustaining power of the presence of God. Perhaps the greatest prophet of the Old Testament is in such despair that he considers his own death, but in the depths of that despair he encounters the grace and presence of God.

This is how it is for many Christians who have unresolved issues stemming from childhood sexual abuse and who find themselves as adults acting in inappropriate ways on the Internet. By all outward appearances they are devoted to their faith, and some are considered by others to be pillars of the Christian community. And to a great extent they are good, Christian people. But they have a dark secret hidden behind the closed doors of their private lives. And when there current behavior is exposed and are simultaneously confronted by the reality of their past abuse, many of them ask, "How will I ever have the strength to face it?" Overwhelmed with embarrassment and shame, fear and anxiety, some wonder where they will ever find the strength to survive. Some, like Jeff, even contemplate suicide.

In the midst of Elijah's crisis, God sent an angel. And to those whose lives are in crisis due to a blend of current cybersexual behaviors and a past of sexual abuse, God too sends his angels.

In both Hebrew and Greek, the language of the Old and New Testaments, the word for angels is translated as "messenger." References to God's messengers are sprinkled throughout the Bible. The strangers who appeared at Abraham and Sarah's tent to tell her she would bear a son in her old age were angels (messengers) from God. Gabriel was the angel who delivered the message to the Virgin Mary that she would conceive a child. Soon after, the shepherds who watched over their flocks by night were heralded with a message from divine messengers. And at the empty tomb an angel delivered the message of Jesus' resurrection.

For those like Jeff who despaired of his circumstances, the message of the Bible is clear: keep your eyes open for "angels unaware." For those in the depths of despair, the question is: are there angels in your life? Can you see God's messengers operating in your life? Are you paying attention enough to see them?

Perhaps God is using *you* as one of his messengers. You may not be aware of it, but perhaps God is using you as a messenger of grace. Perhaps it is you who will provide comfort, like the angel who ministered to Elijah beneath his tree. Perhaps God will use you to bring messages of hope when a friend struggles with past trauma. Or perhaps God is using you as a guardian angel, helping to care and protect a loved one from the dangers of the Internet.

Up on Mount Horeb, the angel of the Lord provided food and water for Elijah. Whether we are God's angels ministering to those who struggle, or whether we are the ones being ministered unto, the grace of God provides us all not just bread, but the bread of life and not just water, but the living water of Christ. For as Jesus said, "Whoever drinks the water that I give will never thirst."

Renewal and Restoration:
The Process Begins

The first step in recovery is to admit one is a victim of abuse and pray for healing. The impact of abuse does not go away by trying to block it out or forget it. That actually makes it worse. It's best to deal directly with the abuse. Christians have an advantage when dealing with abuse. God understands and helps heal the inner pain. In Jeff's case, he finally broke the code of silence. This was a very important step in his healing. Yes, he was afraid. He was afraid of waking old and bad feelings related to the abuse that he tried to silence by keeping the secret, but the feelings were always close. By confronting the abuse, he empowered himself. He often felt hopeless and helpless to make the abuse stop when he was younger. He was not going to let fear rule him any longer. Sometimes talking about one's abuse is like reliving it emotionally. It hurts. Some cry and weep. Some get very angry. These are all normal feelings and reactions and are healthy to experience. This is the path to take to help lessen the powerful grip of negative feelings and emotions, the ones kept repressed or denied. It may hurt at first, but over time, people start to feel better. They've released this emotion that has been trapped for so long. Jeff broke the silence and started talking and feeling. He cried too. It took time for him to work through all these emotions, but eventually he started feeling better and more in control.

The first person Jeff disclosed his abuse to was his counselor. This occurred once he experienced the counselor to be a safe person. Since Jeff was abused by a male and his counselor was male, it took time for Jeff to trust him. His betrayal of trust was a key dynamic in his victimization. Rebuilding trust by taking a chance or risk was an important step. He had a desire to be understood and not shamed for his past. When his confidence grew, he took another important step in healing. He talked to his mother and father and told them of the abuse. They were supportive and non-judgmental. His fears of rejection and shame did not come true, and his progress in rebuilding trust took another step forward.

Jeff began to understand how his abuse had affected his life. His story was a sad and painful one. He took the time to talk and think about this issue. He was able to realize his abuse was a major factor in his history of depression and social anxiety, and specifically how it impacted his desire for pornography. He began to take steps to improve his self-esteem and social confidence. This process took time. There are no hard and fast rules on how long the healing process should take. Each person approaches healing at his own pace. At The Hope and Recovery Institute, clients are never forced to talk about painful memories and emotions.

Abuse sometimes damages one's ability to believe in and trust God. We call this spiritual abuse. It's hard to trust an authority figure like God when one's been traumatized by an authority figure, especially if the offender is a proclaimed Christian. Jeff found comfort in God, but it took time for him to develop confidence in God. Initially, he was angry with God. He thought God should have protected him from the abuse. He believed God should intervene and prevent children from abuse. He thought God abandoned him and must have hated him because of the abuse and resulting problems he developed. He was angry and too ashamed to talk with God for a very long time. Jeff tempted God during the dark days of his depression and sexual acting out. As he drove home from work, he'd drive fast and close his eyes. He would then open them after a few seconds. He theorized that if he got in an accident, then God was out to punish him. When no accident occurred, then God must not be angry with him and wanted to spare his life. Jeff repeated this deadly game day after day.

One day while driving, Jeff hit an ice patch and slid off the road into the ditch. No one was hurt. A kind elderly person came to his rescue. This made an impression on Jeff. He was scared, but someone reached out to him in his time of need. He doesn't recall the name of that gentleman, but he'll never forget that moment in time. It woke him up. He realized it was a close call, a wake-up call. He never played this game again.

Looking back, Jeff can realize how he was so low and depressed in his life that he wanted to die. But he didn't really want to die. He wanted to be rescued, to be saved, to be free from his inner turmoil and years of pain. He felt imprisoned. Child abuse can be so traumatic. It affects how people feel about themselves and how they view the world. It is much more than just the physical act of the sexual abuse. It's the resulting emotional pain and confusion and the damage it can do in the innocent and trusting mind of a child. The abuse caused Jeff to be angry with God for years. Now that he is a committed Christian, he understands child abuse is a product of evil and that God is love and healing.

Jeff continues to make progress in his life to this day. He is still in counseling, now active in his church, and hoping to marry. He has come such a long way. He has fought any temptation to return to the evils of pornography. It almost cost him his life— physically, emotionally, and spiritually. But he has broken the cycle of abuse. He disclosed it, talked about it, and understood the impact it was having on his life. He now trusts God and is no longer angry. He has tried to forgive his offender, but this will take more time. Healing takes time, and those supporting victims like Jeff need to be patient.

If you are a victim of any type of abuse—sexual, physical, mental, or spiritual—you are not alone. There are many who have suffered and can understand how you might feel. Jeff found the light out of the darkness. He found a spiritual path that led him out of the wilderness. Jeff's story is sad and painful, but it is also a story of hope. God will give you what you need to take this journey as well. He knows every child that suffers. He's watching and he's always ready and willing to help. He wants his children healed and happy. Trust God, and good things will happen.

Strategies for Renewal

Admission and talking about and understanding one's abuse are the hallmarks of abuse recovery. This leads to empowerment and hope. The following interventions are designed to help victims identify and express their feelings about their abuse and their abuser.

A Letter Destroyed

Write a letter to your offender, but don't send it to him. Write down all your thoughts and feelings. Say whatever you want to say. Use whatever words you want to use to express yourself. It's your letter. He will never read or see it. You can be as free as you want in your expression. Talk about your anger. Talk about your hurt. Talk about how the abuse has affected you. If you want the offender to go to jail or prison, tell him that, too. Don't hold back on saying what you are moved to say. Give yourself permission to cut loose and tell it like it is. These are your feelings. Maybe you've never been able to tell your offender exactly how you feel, but now you can. This is a safe way to express yourself. It helps organize your thoughts and feelings about your offense. It is an outlet for self-expression. You are no longer a victim. You have the power, control, and right to say whatever you want.

Hold onto the letter for a day or two, or for as long as you want. Then rip it up. Destroy it. Get rid of it. This is a symbolic gesture that the abuse is over and you will no longer be held captive to it. Many people feel better getting their feelings out in this way. It might be helpful to you if you still struggle with some aspect of the abuse.

A Letter Sent

This intervention is very similar to the one above. It's more confrontational, and sometimes victims feel uncomfortable taking this step. It's more risky if you're unsure how the offender may react. Some may get angry. Some may be very understanding. Often, people are more careful with what they say or how they say it. They are more restrained. You have to do what's right for you. If sending a letter feels uncomfortable or unsafe, then it's probably better not to send it.

A Phone Call

Talking to one's offender on the phone is a more direct form of communication. Some like this approach while others feel too intimidated and do not want to hear the offender's voice. This is more personal, but again, one cannot always predict how the offender will react. Some write down what they want to say because it's easier. Anxiety is common when taking this step. The bottom line: if you feel unsafe or highly anxious, this step is probably not for you.

Face-to-Face Contact

This step involves talking to the offender and expressing one's self directly. Most victims pick a place to meet where they feel safe. This can include a public place. Some take a support person along. They can sit in on the conversation or wait in the car. Whatever the victim feels right about doing should be done. Safety is always the first priority. It's difficult to talk to someone directly about abuse if they are the offender. This is a very difficult step for many to take, and usually completed only after the victim has gone to counseling, and the counselor has helped prepare the victim for such an encounter.

An Invitation to Counseling

Inviting the offender to counseling can be a very rewarding and healing experience. However, most offenders are resistant to this invitation. The counselor helps establish safety within the confines of the therapy office and decides with the victim the purpose and goals of the session. By letter or phone call, the offender is typically invited to a counseling session by the victim. A phone call can occur from the counselor's office. The counselor can also play a role in constructing the letter. Even if the offender rejects the invitation, a progressive step has occurred because it takes courage to take this type of step in the first place. It's a form of empowerment.

A WORD FROM JEFF'S MOM

When my husband and I first found out Jeff had been arrested, we were shocked and dumbfounded. We did not raise our son to get in trouble with the law. We were hurt, angry, confused, sad, and scared. We knew Jeff had always had some struggles socially, but we hoped he would just grow out of it. We had no clue he had been sexually abused.

I cried for days when he first told us. I could not sleep, and I just kept picturing him getting abused. This all seemed like a bad dream. We could not understand why he never told us what happened. I've always been overly protective and I couldn't fathom how it had happened right under my nose. Moreover, I couldn't understand why anyone would want to hurt him like that.

I did not realize how frightened he was of his offender and how his fear and shame affected him so deeply. I also had no clue as to the potential dangers of the Internet, especially all the pornography out there. It is very frightening to think how many kids are involved in this type of problem without parents knowing what's going on.

I'm glad Jeff's secret about his abusive past and pornography addiction is now out in the open. He went to counseling and has made a lot of progress. I know it's been a painful process for him—for us as well—but he's done a lot of growing up over the past few years. He had strayed from church, but now attends regularly. And his girlfriend seems really nice and supportive of him. Suicidal thinking, abuse, addiction, and legal trouble: these are a parent's worst nightmare. But now there is hope where there was once despair. That's something to be thankful for.

A LETTER
FROM JEFF'S COUNSELOR

Jeff was referred to me for counseling by his attorney. I've worked with Jeff for over three years and have gotten to know him quite well. At the onset of counseling, Jeff was quiet and soft-spoken. It was difficult for him to talk openly about his thoughts and feelings. He was very suspicious and mistrustful. He suffered from low self-esteem and self-confidence. It was obvious Jeff did not like himself very much. As Jeff began to trust me more, he felt safe enough to share his life story. This was both a painful yet rewarding journey of self-discovery. Jeff revealed he had a secret he'd safeguarded for years. He'd never told anyone this secret.

One day, Jeff disclosed that he was sexually abused by a baby-sitter when he was a child. He told his story over a period of months, sharing only what he felt comfortable sharing during any given session. He described in vivid detail how he was abused. He was haunted by memories he could not get out of his head. Sometimes he cried and at other times he became angry. He blamed himself and questioned why he was targeted for abuse. He was also angry with himself. He felt he should have made the abuse stop. He felt he should have been strong and tough. He felt he had done something to encourage the offender.

Jeff has made significant progress in changing his view of the abuse. He realizes he was a child and the abuse was not his fault. This was a big therapeutic step. He still gets angry with the offender and sometimes thinks of the abuse. But he also understands this is a normal part of the healing process.

Jeff wrote a letter to his offender. This took months to complete. For so long he'd kept silent; he wasn't sure what to write. He crafted a letter expressing his anger. He read the letter out loud during a counseling session. After feeling some anger, and crying a tear, he ripped up the letter. This was to symbolize he was no longer a prisoner of abuse. He felt he had confronted his offender, letting out feelings that needed to be vented. He took some power back.

Jeff is still my client. I'm very proud of the progress he's made. He's developed into a fine young man. His journey has been long and difficult, but well worth it.

Dancing on the Edge of a Cliff

The Legal Risk of Viewing Child Pornography

ERIC'S STORY

Three thunderous knocks echoed through my house. I jumped up, grabbed my bathrobe, and hurried downstairs. Pulling the curtains aside, I cautiously peeked out the window. Two men dressed in dark suits stood ominously on my doorstep. I opened the door a crack as one man flashed a silver badge that read, "Federal Bureau of Investigation," and then asked, "Are you Mr. Smith?" With my heart pounding, I nervously nodded yes. The agent replied, "We need to talk."

■ ■ ■

I struggled for a very long time with my decision to talk about my problem with Internet pornography. I felt so much embarrassment and shame. But after considerable thought, prayer, and encouragement from a counselor, I decided I would take this step and talk about it. My counselor suggested that writing my story might be therapeutic because it's a way to help others learn from my mistakes. This is my story.

My problem with pornography dates back to when I was a teenager. My father had numerous pornographic magazines hidden in his bedroom closet. I found them one day when borrowing one of his ties for church. I looked through all the pages one by one, not wanting to miss a single picture. I was hooked immediately.

I felt sexually aroused and excited when I looked at naked people. It is the same type of feeling drug addicts and alcoholics experience when they get high. I got high on pornography instead of drugs. Many people may find this hard to believe; I was skeptical at first, too. I had no idea one could get addicted to pornography.

My addiction to pornographic magazines led to an addiction to pornographic movies. Prior to marriage, I had a collection of movies and magazines. When I got married, I knew pornography should not be a part of a Christian home so I got rid of them. Despite doing this, my craving for pornography did not subside. My struggle to control these cravings was a tough battle. I prayed for change and spiritual renewal, and there were times when I'd go without pornography for weeks and even months. I'd feel a sense of confidence that I was in control of this evil, but then the feelings and urges to use would return.

There were many times I didn't even care about stopping the craving to use again. The feelings were so strong I just couldn't help myself. I'd tell myself I wasn't really hurting anyone and that there were people who did worse things than I was doing. After all, I was a good provider, worked on my marriage, and most people probably thought I was a good parent as well. I never cheated on my wife, unless you counted the pornography.

What caused me to use? Sometimes I was bored with the physical aspect of my marriage. Sometimes, the stress of living would get to me and I'd need a release or escape. Other times, my desire for pornography would come out of the blue and I'd have no clue what triggered it. I think it became so habitual that I didn't need a reason to use.

I continued this pattern for years, never gaining control of it. I just didn't know how to stop. When we bought a faster computer and hooked up to the Internet, my situation worsened. I discovered pornography was everywhere online. I never paid for it, as most of it was free. There were pictures and pornography sites that captured any type of sexual interest or desire. I spent hours exploring, surfing one site after another. I downloaded and saved hundreds of pictures to my hard drive. I started to collect them.

My exploration of the Internet led to the discovery of chatrooms. These are online rooms where people gather to talk about sexual themes and explore fantasies. Each room can contain as few as two people, or as many as thirty or more. You can type whatever you want in the room, or just sit back and watch others interact. These chatrooms have different kinds of titles or themes. The name of the room tells you the type of conversation you're likely to encounter there. Themes include' cheating on wives and husbands,' ' incest,' 'sex with children,' 'sex with animals,' you name it. There are even Christian-themed rooms. I visited all these rooms out of curiosity. Sometimes I chatted in the rooms, talked about one of my many fantasies, or just watched others chat about their sexual fantasies. I found it exciting and arousing.

I started to trade pictures I had collected from the Internet with other males I met in chatrooms. I didn't know their ages or names. It was called "anonymous trading." Even though free pictures were abundant on the online, there was something exciting about trading with others. We discussed the pictures using sexual descriptions. Some men even find "trading partners." This means finding someone to trade with on a regular basis. This is common for men who trade pictures of their wives. It's also common to trade with people who have other similar interests. For example, men who enjoy pictures of young children find men with similar interests.

There are numerous chatrooms devoted to trading pictures of young girls. The age of the young girl is usually not specified because it could attract unwanted attention from the authorities, meaning the police. It could mean trading pictures of girls in their twenties, teens, or even younger. I ventured into chatrooms with the young girl theme, and before long I put my name on something called a "list." A list is started by someone in the chatroom. The goal is for everyone to share one picture with all group members. In return, one will get a picture from everyone else on the list. It is a quick way to get pictures from others who share your interest. The person who sets up the list has software that allows him to collect and distribute the pictures to all the group members. The provider of the list instructs group members and simply asks who wants to be on the list. A simple response of "Yes I do," is all that is required. You send a picture from your own collection to the "list provider," and pictures are quickly distributed to all people on the list. There is no way to verify the age of anyone who chooses to participate. This means children and teenagers can get on a list and receive pornographic pictures.

Several times I received pictures in a chatroom that were of very young children; some were totally naked, while others were engaged in sexual acts with adults or other children. My first response was, This must be wrong, and I deleted them right away. However, I kept going back to chatrooms and putting my name on lists. I kept getting pictures of young children and began to become more curious about them. I justified my behavior by telling myself I wasn't really hurting anyone; they were just pictures after all. My initial concerns about the legality of what I was doing began to fade over time.

Consequently, I saved several pictures on my computer of young children. I started to trade these pictures with other men and they gave me pictures they had collected. I did not know these men. One day, I traded several pictures of naked young teen girls to a man I had never met before in a chatroom. That was my final trade. The next day, two agents appeared on my doorstep and I was arrested for possessing child pornography on my computer hard drive.

My arrest shocked my wife and family. I was embarrassed and ashamed. Yet that moment changed my life for the better. It was a blessing in disguise. I had to face the painful truth that I had become addicted to pornography, hid the problem for a long time, and was not living up to the moral standards I had set for myself and family. It felt like I had fallen from grace.

I was processed through the legal system. It was an emotional nightmare. I had to hire an attorney, go through a psychological evaluation, seek counseling, and eventually be sentenced in court. My name and picture now appear on my state's sex offender registry. This whole ordeal has changed my life forever.

There are many men dancing on the edge of the cliff. Many good men flirt with disaster and potential legal consequences. I'm not a pedophile. I'm not a sexual predator. I don't think of children in sexual ways. I became addicted to online adult pornography and did not get in control of this problem until it was too late. It was never my intention to look at or download pictures of children onto my computer. I would never harm a child in any way. Don't take a chance with your life. Get pornography out of your life before it's too late.

Risky Business:
Dancing on the Edge of a Cliff

How can this happen? How does someone go from looking at and desiring adult pornography to desiring child pornography? Most men who look at child pornography should not be confused with sexual predators or pedophiles. They are not necessarily emotionally or sexually attracted to children. They have no craving or desire for children. They do not make up sexual fantasies about children.

Most people believe child pornography is morally wrong. Most men who struggle with adult pornography believe child pornography is wrong, too. So how do men like Eric get to a point where, despite knowing looking at children is morally wrong, they look anyway?

Part of the problem is that child pornography is more available on the Internet than people realize, and unfortunately, it's easy to find. Web sites, chatrooms, trading groups, and shareware make access to child pornography easy and tempting.

Some men are curious about child pornography but are not motivated by sexual desires for children. However, if curiosity is accompanied by some sexual arousal, even if the arousal is minimal at first, the risk of developing a growing desire for child pornography increases.

For many men, looking at adult pornography puts them in a sexually charged or aroused state, physically and mentally. If child pornography is viewed during this time, then pleasure is once again associated with child pornography. The desire to look again is then reinforced unless the individual quickly turns away from the pornography, thus stopping the arousal before it becomes stronger. It's a form of conditioning. Pleasure is a powerful dynamic and type of reinforcement. Morals against looking at child pornography begin to fade, and the individual often rationalizes his behavior. What may start out as curiosity begins to evolve into a pattern of desire reinforced by looking at child pornography and experiencing pleasure.

An individual can obtain online child pornography and get into legal trouble in many ways, including:

- Trading child pornography to an undercover federal agent or police officer

- Trading child pornography to someone he believes is trustworthy, but who then reports him to the authorities

- Purchasing online child pornographic material from undercover federal authorities

- Buying child pornography from a manufacturer or distributor who is later arrested and whose distributor's list leads the authorities to him

- Trading pornography openly on the Internet through shareware and trading groups, which can be infiltrated by the authorities

The Legal Implications
of Child Pornography

The possession of child pornography is illegal. This includes pornographic pictures or movies saved or stored on one's computer hard drive or onto computer discs.

Many incorrectly assume that deleting this material after looking at it erases it from the computer. Actually, the material is still saved on the computer's hard drive. The authorities have sophisticated software that recaptures the pictures believed to have been deleted. Imagine the shock and surprise some experience when pictures begin showing up on their computer's monitor during an investigation. Once these pictures appear, they can be used as evidence resulting in criminal charges under state and federal laws.

Frank Stanley is an experienced criminal defense lawyer in Grand Rapids, Michigan, who, among other things, specializes in the defense of individuals charged by federal or state authorities with any type of involvement with child pornography.[2] He shares his legal expertise below to help you better understand the potential legal ramifications of possessing child pornography.

Defining the Crime

Laws governing the investigation and prosecution of child pornography vary from state to state, but looking at Michigan's law will help illustrate the point that breaking these laws is a serious matter.

In Michigan, child pornography is called "child sexually abusive material." A *child* is defined as "a person who is less than eighteen years of age." This creates an interesting anomaly in that Michigan's age of consent is sixteen. In Michigan, it would be legally permissible to have consensual sex with a sixteen-year-old but legally impermissible to photograph or record the sexual act.

The Prevalence of Child Pornography on the Internet[1]

- Demand for pornographic images of babies and toddlers on the Internet is soaring. Moreover, the images are becoming more graphically violent and disturbing.

- The typical age of children is between six and twelve, but that profile is getting younger.

- Approximately twenty new children appear on porn sites every month, many of them kidnapped or sold into the pornography industry.

- More than 20,000 images of child pornography are posted on the Internet every week.

- According to researchers who monitored the Internet over a six-week period, more than 140,000 pornographic images of children were posted. Twenty children appearing in these images were estimated to have been abused for the first time, and more than 1,000 images of each child were created.

- Child pornography generates $3 billion annually.

Child sexually abusive material is defined as "a child engaging in a listed sexual act." *Listed sexual act* is defined as "sexual intercourse, erotic fondling, sadomasochistic abuse, masturbation, passive sexual involvement, sexual excitement, or erotic nudity."

Erotic fondling is defined as "touching a person's clothed or unclothed genitals, pubic area, buttocks, or, if the person is a female, breasts, or if the person is a child, the developing or undeveloped breast area, for the purpose of real or simulated overt sexual gratification or stimulation." Physical contact that is not for the purpose of sexual gratification or stimulation is expressly excluded from the definition.

Passive sexual involvement is defined as "a real or simulated act that is designed to expose another person to or draws another person's attention to one of the listed acts for the purpose of real or simulated overt sexual gratification or stimulation."

Erotic nudity is defined as "the lascivious exhibition of genital, pubic, or rectal area of any individual." *Lascivious* is in turn defined as "wanton, lewd, lustful, and tending to produce voluptuous or lewd emotion."

Federal Law

Federal law also criminalizes child pornography along with other specific crimes involving children, for example, interstate transportation of a child for an illicit purpose. Because Michigan and the federal government are two separate sovereigns, either or both jurisdictions could prosecute a person who violates the statute.

The definitional section under federal law speaks in terms of a depiction of "a minor engaging in sexually explicit conduct."

A *minor* is defined as "any person under the age of eighteen." However, different states may have different ages of consent for females and males.

Child pornography is defined as "any visual depiction, including any photograph, film, video, picture, or computer, or computer-generated image or picture, whether made or produced by electronic, mechanical, or other means of sexually explicit conduct."

Sexually explicit conduct is defined as including "graphic sexual intercourse of whatever type and whatever gender of the participants." This definition includes lascivious simulated sexual intercourse where the genitals, breast, or pubic area of any individual is exhibited. It also includes graphic depictions of lascivious simulated bestiality, masturbation, or sadistic or masochistic abuse and/or the graphic or simulated exhibition of the genitals or pubic area of any person.

Graphic means that "a viewer can observe any part of the genitals or pubic area of any depicted person, during any part of the time that sexually explicit conduct is being depicted."

Visual depiction is defined as including "undeveloped film and videotape, and the data stored on the computer disc or by electronic means which is capable of conversion into a visual image."

Once the authorities determine whether a picture on one's computer qualifies as child pornography, a decision is made as to whether or not the individual has committed a crime. For example, Michigan identifies three tiers of conduct. Each tier is subject to a different penalty. Each tier requires the person to "know, have reason to know, or should be reasonably expected to know" that the depiction is a depiction of a child. A person who does not take reasonable precautions to determine the age of someone depicted can be criminally implicated even if that person did not think the image depicted a child.

Tier One: The first tier includes anyone who "persuades, induces, entices, coerces, causes, or knowingly allows a child to engage in child sexually abusive activity for the purpose of producing any child sexually abusive material." This is commonly understood to be someone who has direct contact with the child whose images are being recorded. One published Michigan case involved one minor photographing two other minors having sex with one another.

The statute also includes in the first tier "a person who arranges for, produces, makes, or finances, or a person who attempts, prepares or conspires to arrange for, produce, make, or finance any child sexually abusive activity or child sexually abusive material."

A recent Michigan Court of Appeals case held that someone that would otherwise be a simple possessor (Tier 3) could be prosecuted as a Tier 1 violator. In that case, the individual downloaded images from the Internet onto CDRs. The CDRs were not disseminated to anyone else. They were intended as a means of storage. Nevertheless, because the individual had copied the images onto the CDRs, the Court considered him to be a producer. This was deemed true even though the individual had never had contact with the child depicted and didn't know the child's identity.

Tier Two: The second tier includes a person who "distributes, promotes or finances the distribution or promotion or receives for the purposes of distribution or promotion, or conspires, attempts, or prepares to distribute, receive, finance, or promote any child sexually abusive material." This tier has historically included individuals who disseminate the images to others. This tier could include the original creators of the pornography. It also could include those individuals who obtain the images from whatever sources and distribute them to others. It also includes people that finance the distribution operation.

Tier Three: The third tier includes a person who knowingly possesses any child sexually abusive material. This tier has historically included the end-user, that is, an individual who possesses the material for personal reasons who had nothing to do with the original creation of the material and who does not disseminate the material to any third party.

Consequences: Federal or State Prison

Both Michigan and the federal government use sentencing guidelines to compute a sentencing range. The Michigan guidelines are presently mandatory. The federal guidelines are supposedly advisory, but they are quasi-mandatory since most sentences are imposed within those guidelines. The federal penalties are much more severe than the Michigan penalties. In a recent example, an individual who was convicted by a federal court for possession of child pornography received a 14 year sentence. Had that individual been prosecuted in a Michigan state court, the minimum sentence would have been approximately 3 years.

There are numerous variables that impact the type of punishment and help the authorities determine the seriousness of the consequences. For example, age of child, number of pornographic images involved, use of the computer, and number of victims are all examined very carefully by the authorities. Prison is a very real punishment for the possession of child pornography.

Mr. Stanley's articulation of state and federal law regarding the possession of child pornography should strike fear into anyone who has child pornography of any kind and any form in their possession. Remember, deleting pictures from one's hard drive does not really delete them; they are still there. Even if the pictures were technically deleted years ago, it can still be interpreted as possessing child pornography. This is very chilling news for those who believe they are protected from prosecution. The above information is also a wake-up call for those experimenting with or curious about child pornography.

From Investigation to Conviction

When an individual is investigated and subsequently arrested for the possession of child pornography, the process of protecting one's legal rights is expensive, time-consuming, and socially embarrassing. There are several steps involved in the legal process.

Investigation: When the state and/or federal authorities have reason to believe someone may have broken the law regarding child pornography, they can launch an investigation of the individual. The individual becomes a suspect in the commission of a crime.

It is common for the authorities to request an examination of the individual's computer in their own home, or obtain a warrant for an arrest or a search. Many times, the authorities want to talk to the individual without an attorney present in the hopes of finding evidence and getting a confession. A confession is given verbally, but may also be written and signed by the suspect. This makes the case much stronger and easier to prosecute. Once a confession is given, the individual loses leverage in his ability to negotiate a favorable legal resolution.

Legal Counsel: An attorney who is hired by the suspect requires money in exchange for legal representation. This is called a "retainer." Suspects who cannot afford legal representation may be assigned a court-appointed attorney. Legal representation can be very expensive. Legal fees can run into the thousands of dollars. The cost will vary depending on the complexity of the case and the attorney's time commitment. The cost can also vary depending on whether the case is prosecuted by the state or federal authorities. Legal fees are much higher in federal prosecutions because of the greater complexity of federal law. Most suspects are shocked by the costs, and yet there is no guarantee spending thousands of dollars can alter the outcome of the suspect's legal fate.

Arrest: If a suspect is arrested, he now becomes a defendant in a legal case against him. The arrest can take place at home or even at work. This means the possibility of being handcuffed in front of one's children or coworkers and escorted to a police car for all to see. This step can be very intimidating and traumatic for all who witness the arrest.

The defendant is typically sent to jail and placed in a holding cell with other defendants. Fingerprints and pictures are taken by the police. The individual is placed in a holding cell until he goes to court for an arraignment. The charges are read in front of a judge, and the judge determines if the defendant will be released from jail on bond. This requires a sum of money determined by the judge. The defendant remains out of jail until final sentencing, or until some condition of the bond is broken, for example, looking at child pornography.

Many months can elapse from the beginning of an investigation to prosecution and ultimately sentencing. There are additional court hearings, meeting with attorneys and the probation department, and most likely a referral for a psychological evaluation and/or counseling. Sometimes the evaluation is referred to as a "sexual deviancy" evaluation.

Evaluations: Psychological/sexual deviancy evaluations can be requested by the defendant's attorney or ordered by the authority of the court. These evaluations are conducted by professionals who have credentials and expertise in this area. A typical evaluation includes a series of clinical interviews and psychological testing.

The goal of such interviews is to:

- Learn as much as possible about why the defendant was involved with child pornography
- Assess whether the defendant exhibits any genuine remorse for his actions
- Assess relapse potential
- Assess amenability to treatment and which kind will be most beneficial
- Determine whether the defendant is a pedophile or sexual predator
- Address any question the attorney or court poses in the referral question, such as whether the defendant exhibits any signs of mental illness

The goal of psychological testing is to collect additional "data" or information on the defendant. This can include assessment of the defendant's intellectual functioning, emotional and personality attributes, sexual deviancy attitudes, psychological/physical arousal patterns to children, and in general, the defendant's overall mental health. This step also takes time and money to complete. The evaluator collects all the information and writes a report on the defendant. This report can be used by the court in determining the defendant's sentence.

Until an individual decides to plead guilty or is convicted after trial, care must be taken to protect the information shared between the psychological professional and the individual being evaluated. This confidentiality can be assured through one or more privileges, e.g. the lawyer/client privilege and/or the doctor/patient privilege. However, since the law varies from jurisdiction to jurisdiction, it is important that the confidentiality issue be addressed at the outset of the evaluation process.

Counseling: The defendant is referred to counseling by his attorney or by the court as a part of his sentencing. Counseling may include individual counseling or group counseling with other men who have some type of sexual deviancy problem. The goal of counseling is to try to understand, in as much detail as possible, why the defendant committed the crime. This means talking about and understanding what events in the defendant's life affected his curiosity, desire, and/or addiction to use pornography, and specifically child pornography. Counseling can take a year or more in most cases. It also costs money, and the court often wants to know how the defendant is progressing in counseling. The counselor may have to write a letter to the probation department each month with this type of update.

The Day of Judgment: Finally, after many months and much anxiety and expense, the day of sentencing arrives. The defendant, along with his attorney, stands in front of the judge. The courtroom is likely to be filled with other defendants awaiting their sentences, family members, and other interested parties. The judge makes the final decision or judgment about the defendant's legal fate. Prison, jail, fines, probation, community service, loss of computer privileges, and inclusion on the state sex offender registry are all possible legal consequences. Loss of family, job, and notoriety in the newspaper can change how the defendant is viewed and treated by the community for the rest of his life.

It is a sobering moment in the lives of many offenders. Defendants often have no real idea or clue as to the seriousness of their crime in the eyes of the community and court. If a law is broken, the court must respond accordingly. Hearing the judge's proclamation of "Mr. Smith, you are hereby sentenced to the Jackson Correctional Facility for a period of three to five years" is a powerful dose of reality.

Criminal Penalties

Mr. Stanley outlines the potential legal consequences or penalties associated with child pornography. These penalties may differ depending on the state where the crime is committed. Regardless, these consequences are real and life changing.

Both Michigan and the federal government use sentencing guidelines to compute a sentencing range. The Michigan guidelines are presently mandatory. The federal guidelines are supposedly advisory, but they are quasi-mandatory since most sentences are imposed within those guidelines. A defendant can be charged at both the state and federal level. There are many factors that can influence the penalty assigned to the crime, for example, physical injury to victim, psychological injury to victim, number of victims, criminal sexual penetration, and defendant's criminal history. A very long prison sentence (more than twenty years) is also a possibility under federal guidelines.

In Michigan law, the statutory maximum penalties are:

TIER 1	not more than twenty years
TIER 2	not more than seven years
TIER 3	not more than four years
TIER 1 and computers	not more than twenty years
TIER 2 and computers	not more than ten years
TIER 3 and computers	not more than seven years

In federal law, the defendant is not eligible for parole and will likely serve the sentence imposed, less an allowance for good time. The good time allowance is presently 15% of a person's sentence. Good time is not automatic. It must be earned by good behavior.

In Michigan law, a minimum and a maximum sentence is imposed. The maximum sentence is set by statute. The minimum sentence is set by the Court. The minimum sentence is a parole eligibility date. However, eligibility is not the same as entitlement, and many Michigan prisoners serve well beyond their minimum dates.

Scriptural Guidance
for Keeping Your Balance

There is a clear distinction between legal pornography and child pornography, which has profound legal consequences. Unfortunately, many men fail to notice that they are getting dangerously close to the edge of legality. It is as if they are dancing on the edge of a cliff. And if they do not exercise control and restraint, they risk plummeting to the valley of serious legal and personal consequences.

For those men, inspiration can be found in the following episode of the life of the prophet Ezekiel:

> *The hand of the Lord was upon me, and he brought me out by the Spirit of the Lord and set me in the middle of a valley; it was full of bones. He led me back and forth among them, and I saw a great many bones on the floor of the valley, bones that were very dry. He asked me, "Son of man, can these bones live?"*
>
> *I said, "O Sovereign Lord, you alone know."*
>
> *Then he said to me, "Prophesy to these bones and say to them, 'Dry bones, hear the word of the Lord. This is what the Sovereign Lord says to these bones: I will make breath enter you, and you will come to life. I will attach*

tendons to you and make flesh come upon you and cover you with skin; I will put breath in you, and you will come to life. Then you will know that I am the Lord."

So I prophesied as I was commanded. And as I was prophesying, there was a noise, a rattling sound, and the bones came together, bone to bone. I looked, and tendons and flesh appeared on them and skin covered them, but there was no breath in them.

Then he said to me, "Prophesy to the breath; prophesy, son of man, and say to it, 'This is what the Sovereign Lord says: Come from the four winds, O breath, and breathe into these slain, that they may live.'" So I prophesied as he commanded me, and breath entered them; they came to life and stood up on their feet—a vast army.

Then he said to me: "Son of man, these bones are the whole house of Israel. They say, 'Our bones are dried up and our hope is gone; we are cut off.' Therefore, prophesy and say to them, 'This is what the Sovereign Lord says: O my people, I am going to open your graves and bring you up from them; I will bring you back to the land of Israel. Then you, my people, will know that I am the Lord, when I open your graves and bring you up from them. I will put my Spirit in you and you will live, and I will settle you in your own land. Then you will know that I, the Lord, have spoken, and I have done it, declares the Lord.'"

EZEKIEL 37:1–14, NIV

There is tremendous hope to be found in this text from the prophecy of Ezekiel. The context is the Babylonian captivity; the ancient Israelites were being held captive in Babylon. With their situation seeming to be hopeless, the people lamented, *"Our bones are dried up and our hope is gone."* But God orders the prophet Ezekiel to prophesy to the bones and tell them they are going to live again. The Lord God said, *"I am going to open your graves and bring you up from them; I will bring you back to the land of Israel."*

That was an important message to the people of Israel, a people held in captivity in Babylon. And it is an important message for those who have been held captive by a life of cyber-sex and pornography. This is a message of hope and renewal for those who look around their lives and see only decay and believe, like the Israelites, that their situation is hopeless.

Prior to the Babylonian captivity, Israel had been stubborn and disobedient, bowing down and worshipping other gods. As punishment, God allowed Israel to be taken captive to Babylon, which became a "graveyard" for the people. At times their conditions were bearable, but most often they were oppressed. They couldn't build their life in the foreign land and they couldn't go home. After twenty years away from home, the Israelites began to lose hope. They started asking some fundamental questions like, *Where is God? Why hasn't God delivered us? Why is this happening to us?*

According to Psalm 137, the people were so distraught; they couldn't even sing the songs of their faith that they loved so much. They had hung up their harps and sat bitter and despondent by the banks of the river Chebar. They had lost their land of promise and were unable to experience God's presence. They felt spiritually dead. They felt alone and abandoned.

Perhaps, like the ancient Israelites, you feel spiritually dead. Perhaps you wonder if you can even consider yourself a Christian anymore. You find yourself unable to pray, unable to sing, unable to hope.

Not unlike the ancient Israelites, your spouse also knows what it's like to feel abandoned. Her life has been shattered by your Internet infidelity. She has discovered the extent to which you have been held captive by the dark forces of pornography, and she feels rejected. Your promises to her have been broken, and she too feels hopeless. She may want your marriage to survive, but she laments that it may never be as enjoyable and meaningful as it once was.

The story of Ezekiel reminds us that God was with his exiled people and had compassion for them. God had promised them the land since the time of their father Abraham. The land was important because it gave the Israelites rights, it gave them a home, and it defined them as a nation. God gave the exiles hope that they would return to occupy their land, rebuild their lives, restore their homes, and start anew. God promised to raise their dead spirits from their graves. He commanded Ezekiel to tell the people, *"I will put my Spirit in you, and you will live, and I will settle you in your own land."*

"I will put my Spirit in you," is an important phrase for the Israelites because it speaks of promise, of rebirth, of new life, of hope. In the original Hebrew language of this text, the word "Spirit," or *ru'ah* may also be translated as "wind" or "breath." This word *ru'ah* is a word of life. It is the creative, life-giving force of God. It is a word found in many of the faithful stories of Scripture:

> *In the beginning, God created the heavens and the earth. And the earth was formless and void and the darkness was over the face of the deep; and the Spirit (ru'ah) of God was brooding over the face of the water.*
>
> GEN. 1:1–2, NIV

> *. . . the Lord God formed man of dust from the ground, and breathed into his nostrils the breath (ru'ah) of life; and man became a living being.*
>
> GEN. 2:7, NIV

> *But God remembered Noah and all the beasts and all the cattle that were with him in the ark; and God caused a wind (ru'ah) to pass over the earth, and the water subsided.*
>
> GEN 8:1, NIV

These stories are of creation. Creation out of chaos. Creation with a purpose. Creation given form and life by God alone. And now, once again, the Israelites hear the words of creation: "I am going to open your graves and bring you up from them; I will bring you back to the land of Israel. Then you, my people, will know that I am the Lord, when I open your graves and bring you up from them. I will put my Spirit (ru'ah) in you and you will live."

The promise of renewed life that Ezekiel proclaimed for God is a promise that is still available to you this very day. This passage from Ezekiel brilliantly illustrates the reality that God cares about and helps you in the daily affairs of your life. Like the Israelites in the graveyard called Babylon, you may sometimes feel dead although you are alive. But Ezekiel's vision is a powerful demonstration of God's creative and sustaining love that breathes life back into even the driest of bones.

Strategies for Reestablishing Order

The best way to avoid any legal problems associated with child pornography is to resist looking at, collecting, trading, or saving pictures or movies to your computer's hard drive or discs. It's important to understand the legal risks associated with these types of behaviors. If there are no pictures, there is no crime. There is no fear of investigation and prosecution. Life is more peaceful when you live within the law.

Two interventions can be used to curb the desire for and use of child pornography. These interventions can be used by men who are curious about it, or for those addicted to it.

Reality Therapy

When men are tempted by the desire to look at child pornography, they are encouraged to immediately focus on the legal consequences: jail or prison. This intervention is a form of reality therapy. It focuses on the reality of consequences. The fear of legal consequences can stop any pleasure associated with looking at pornography, because thinking about going to prison is very unpleasant. Such feelings can stop sexual arousal dead in its tracks. Thus, the reality of going to prison can act as a deterrent to using pornography.

Some common consequences associated with using child pornography include:

- Shame and loss of dignity
- Living in fear of legal consequences
- Divorce, loss of family and children
- Legal expense related to criminal defense running into thousands of dollars
- Getting fired at work
- Being identified in the newspaper or television after arrest
- Being placed on the sex offender registry
- Psychological stress (depression, anxiety, fear)
- Jail, prison, probation

Aversive Imagery

Aversive imagery is another technique used to reduce or eliminate undesirable thoughts, fantasies, behaviors, or feelings associated with using child pornography. It involves pairing unwanted thoughts with some type of aversive, or unpleasant, image.

Here's how it works:

Step One: Identify the thoughts, feelings, fantasies, or behaviors that need to be changed. Make a list of them. Common examples include:

- I want to look at child pornography right now.

- I turn on the computer and right away start surfing pornography Web sites. It's only a matter of time before I start looking for pictures of children.

- When I'm at work, I picture myself going home and using the computer for pornography after my wife goes to bed.

- I'm on my favorite sports Web site, and suddenly, my mind drifts to thinking about porn sites.

- I'm sexually frustrated and begin to think of child pictures for excitement and release.

- I'm thinking about children in my mind. I can't get rid of the thoughts.

- I was watching television, when my wife said she had to go to the store. As soon as she left, I went upstairs and started surfing pornography.

Step Two: Identify, stop, and replace these thoughts and feelings with an aversive image. Imagine something very unpleasant. The more graphic and disturbing the image, the better it will work. The goal is to immediately eliminate a thought or feeling which is sexually arousing by replacing it with an image that stops the arousal from getting stronger. For example, imagine being arrested at home in front of your wife and children. The police handcuff, escort, and place you in the police car. You look up and see your children waving good-bye and crying in the front window as the police car drives away.

This aversive image is reality-based because it can and does happen to people. Seeing your children cry and wave good-bye is sad. Those who go through this experience never forget it. It is imprinted on their memory forever. It can be an effective way to stop sexual arousal associated with child pornography. Each individual can construct a unique aversive image that will help them. It takes time to discover what image will be most effective.

Step Three: Practice, practice, and practice some more. This technique needs to be practiced over time for it to be effective. Eventually, an individual will automatically utilize it, and sexual arousal associated with child pornography with be reduced. The reality of legal consequences and aversive imagery can be an effective combination of interventions in combating this problem.

A VIEW FROM A DETECTIVE

I've investigated many cases related to child pornography. When I show up on a suspect's front step and flash my badge, the most common reaction is fear. They reluctantly let me into their home, because my badge carries power and influence.

Most men let me inspect their computers for child pornography. If they resist, I inform them I can obtain a warrant to seize their computers by calling the authorities from their house. I always ask them if I will find something on their computers they should not have, like pictures of children. Some confess to their wrong-doing right away, while others express confidence they do not have anything illegal.

As I check out their computers using special software and pictures begin to surface, some men shake while others cry. It is a very sad moment for them. They know they have done something wrong, and now they have been caught. They usually ask what will happen to them next, and I tell them I need to report these findings to my superiors, but they should think of contacting an attorney.

Reality can be painful, and these men often face jail or prison. Once evidence of a crime has been identified and turned over to my superiors, there is no turning back. Their lives are changed forever.

The Innocent Lambs

On Protecting Our Children

AMY'S STORY

"Mom, come here—hurry! Look at this!"

I jumped out of my seat, peered over Amy's shoulder, and read what someone was typing to her in an instant message. I could not believe my eyes. There, in graphic detail, were proclamations of what this person wanted to do sexually with my daughter. He even wanted to send her a picture of himself naked! I told Amy to shut off the computer immediately. Later that night, we had a long talk.

■ ■ ■

Amy was thirteen when she first started using the Internet. She is our oldest child, so the cyberspace thing was new to us. Like many parents, we bought a computer and connected to the Internet because we thought it would benefit our family, especially our kids. We didn't want them to feel "different" from their friends or have them fall behind in their studies. Amy's teachers encouraged the use of the computer to help with homework. In fact, the kids were required to take computer lab at school. So buying one for our home seemed like the natural thing to do.

Amy began using the Internet right away. She often "talked" online with her friends after school. Sometimes it seemed like she was on the computer all night. But then, our parents complained that we tied up the phone all night when we were teens.

Once in a while, Amy actually used the computer for homework. She could always find what she needed online when researching a topic for a paper or project. It was easier, not to mention quicker, than going to the library like we used to do.

As her time online grew, so did our struggles over the computer. Her dad and I began setting some limits on her usage. Of course, she accused us of "ruining" her social life because of these restrictions.

The night that Amy and I had our long talk, she told me she had seen dirty pictures on the Internet. I was shocked, but calmly asked to know more. She told me they just "popped up" while she was working on a school project. She knew she shouldn't look at them and tried closing out the Web site, but more pictures kept popping up. She had to turn off the computer to make them go away and then restart it. She also told me she's received email from strangers, and sometimes they contained sexual themes. She had no idea how any of them got a hold of her email address.

Amy promised me she's never gone to a pornography site on her own or responded to any of those emails. I was relieved when she told me that. Amy's always been a responsible child and we had no reason not to trust her.

We went into the "history" of received emails on the computer. Amy was right. She had received an email from an unknown source. It was entitled "haven't talked lately." Amy had opened it thinking it was sent by a friend she hadn't talked to in a long time. When we opened it together that night, it immediately linked us to a porn site. Graphic pictures of adults engaging in sex appeared. I was so angry! Who would send such a despicable thing to a child? I didn't want Amy to be exposed to this trash. I decided then that it was time to educate myself more about the dangers of the Internet. Here is some of what I have since discovered.

The Internet is a pornography minefield. Never in my wildest dreams did I imagine the multitudes of pornographic pictures, movies, and Web sites available on the Internet. In fact, if your child is doing research and types in a key word or phrase to search online, it's very possible the list of sites that shows up will contain some links to pornography sites. For example, say your child is doing research on the government and wants information on the White House. One of the sites containing the words "white house" in its domain name was actually a porn site! Pornographers often purchase innocent-sounding or popular domain names to purposefully mislead people to their sites.

Anticipate uninvited guests. Do you realize how easy it is for men to talk to our children online? Some Internet Service Providers (ISPs) offer a membership directory. This allows all subscribers to that ISP to search for other subscribers. Most people, like my Amy, make up a member profile. A profile allows you to describe who you are, your interests, or any other personal information you care to share. Most kids think this is a fun—and harmless—way to communicate with others. However, profiles make it easy for anyone to find your screen name in the directory, read up on your interests, and then send you an instant message.

You've probably read in the newspaper or heard on TV about situations where men use the Internet to contact children. It really does happen, and their intentions are anything but innocent. Some will talk in a very sexual manner to kids. Others will try to win over a child's trust, build up her confidence, and then form an online "relationship."

One mother told me of a situation where her daughter was being stalked online. Every time she signed on, some guy sent her messages, wanting to chat. He'd tell her how sexy and pretty she was and try to get her to chat on the phone. He even sent her a picture of himself. Thank goodness she reported this to her mother and blocked the guy from being able to contact her. But there are lots of children who do not tell their parents, and secret relationships do develop. As a parent, it's frightening to think of the potential dangers. But we need to be aware of them so we can protect our children.

Beware of chatrooms. Another danger to be aware of is chatrooms. Like Web sites, there are some good ones and some not so good ones. They allow people with similar interests to "meet" in a "room" and "talk." (What you see is a real-time dialogue on the screen.) Chatrooms are set up by theme: friends, sports, dating, and so forth. However, some rooms have themes that are sexual in nature. People of all ages, our children included, can access these rooms. But even innocent chatrooms with teen themes are prime targets for pedophiles or predators who are looking for children. Such criminals spend a lot of time thinking of ways to gain access to children. The Internet practically delivers them to their door.

I do not want my daughter or any child exposed to or threatened by these types of people. That's why I've gone to such great lengths to educate my family on the dangers of the Internet. Please educate yourself and your children—before it's too late.

The Internet: A Pedophile's Playground

The Internet can be a dangerous place for our children. The abundance and availability of pornography is mind-boggling. Sexual predators have access to a virtual playground of children. Instead of going to the mall and parks, they can now cruise the Internet looking for vulnerable children to exploit.

Richard B. Maring, CEO of the Tribinium Corporation has devoted himself to protecting children from the dangers of online pornography and predators. His Web site www.seenoevilonline .com provides up-to-date information and resources to combat this international problem. The statistics his organization has gathered are staggering.[1]

- The average age of boys when they are first exposed to pornography on the Internet is eight-and-a-half. For girls, it's eleven.

- Ninety percent of children between the ages of eight and sixteen have viewed online pornography, most while doing homework.

- At least twenty-six children's characters, including Pokeman and Action Man, have been linked to thousands of porn sites.

- Twenty-one percent of teens say they have looked at something on the Internet that they wouldn't want their parents to know about.

- One in five children ages ten to seventeen have received a sexual solicitation over the Internet.

- Three million of the visitors to adult Web sites in September 2000 were under the age of eighteen.

- One in four children who use the Internet are exposed to unwanted sexual material.

- One in seventeen children ages ten to seventeen was threatened or harassed over the Internet in 2000.

- Seventy percent of sexual advances over the Internet happened while youths were on a home computer.

- A survey of 600 households conducted by the National Center of Missing and Exploited Children found that twenty percent of parents do not know any of their children's Internet passwords, instant messaging nicknames, or email addresses.

- Only five percent of parents recognized the acronym POS (parent over shoulder) and only one percent could identify WTGP (want to go private?), both of which are used frequently by teens when instant messaging.

- Incidents of child sexual exploitation have risen from 4,573 cases in 1998 to 112,083 cases in 2004, according to the National Center for Missing and Exploited Children.

- Ninety-six percent of kids have gone online. Seventy-four percent have access at home and sixty-one percent use the Internet on a typical day.
- Twenty percent of youths have received sexual solicitations online. Eighty-nine percent of sexual solicitations were made in chatrooms.

Scriptural Guidance for Helping Our Children Be Faithful Followers of Christ

Hear, O Israel: the Lord our God, the Lord is one. Love the Lord your God with all your heart and with all your soul and with all your strength. These commandments that I give you today are to be upon your hearts. Impress them on your children. Talk about them when you sit at home and when you walk along the road, when you lie down and when you get up. Tie them as symbols on your hands and bind them on your foreheads. Write them on the doorframes of your houses and on your gates.

DEUTERONOMY 6:4–9, NIV

Near the end of four decades of wandering in the desert, the Israelites heard Moses describe what life would be like in the Promised Land. They knew they would be confronted with and impacted by people whose values, lifestyles, and beliefs were altogether different from their own. It was essential that they devise a strategy for surviving as the people of God. And so Moses spoke to the Israelites saying, *"Hear, O Israel: the Lord our God, the Lord is one. Love the Lord your God will all your heart, and with all your soul and with all your strength."*

Persons from the Jewish faith refer to this passage from Deuteronomy as the Shema. It comprises the most important scriptural command of the Jewish faith. Faithful Jews repeat the Shema twice a day, and many have the verse inscribed on the entryway into their homes, reminding them of their faith every time they enter the house.

During his ministry, Jesus referred to this passage as the most important commandment in the entire Bible. As such this text from Deuteronomy serves as the very foundation of what Christians need to teach their children if they are to grow to have a strong faith.

There is much to be learned from these words of Moses: *"You shall love the Lord your God with all your heart, your soul, and your strength."* Your "heart" means your spirit, that part of you that is able to worship and have a relationship with God. Your "soul" includes the rest of your personality—mind, emotions, and will. Your "strength" refers to your physical body. What this verse is saying is that our love for God must consume every part of our being—body, soul, and spirit.

Ever since Moses first spoke those words, people wanting their children to have a vibrant faith in God have followed this command. But Christians who live in the twenty-first century face a particularly difficult challenge because we live within a culture where human relationships and sexuality is debased through pornography. Nonetheless, Moses' words still provide helpful guidance for parents who want their children to grow up in the faith.

The first principal to be learned from this passage is being an example. In verse six, Moses said, *"These commandments that I give you today are to be upon your hearts."* In other words, parents are to model or demonstrate through their own behavior what faithfulness means. This is exceptionally important because children are very impressionable. Children watch their parents and in most cases pattern their own behavior after what they observe. Moreover, children are extremely perceptive and quickly recognize whether there's a correlation between the faith their parents profess and the way their parents live. Children also closely watch and often mimic what they observe in the culture around them. Children want to be seen, especially by their peers, as "cool," "normal," and "acceptable." And that is why the Internet poses such a danger. The Internet contains a vast cultural smorgasbord of what people think is acceptable. But much of it does not meet the standards Christian parents would want to instill in their children.

As a parent, your best defense in this battle for your kids' souls is your example. By your example, have your children learned what it means for a husband and wife to express mutual respect? By your example, have your children learned about marital loyalty and devotion? By your example, have your children learned appropriate affection? By your example, have your children learned that sexuality is to be celebrated within the context of a covenant relationship?

In the seventh verse from this passage, Moses tells us to "Impress [the commandments] on your children." Both the Revised Standard Version and the King James Version translate the Hebrew as "teach diligently," while the New International Version translates it as "impress." The literal meaning of the Hebrew is "to say something twice" or "to repeat." The word originally referred to the sharpening of a blade or a tool by rubbing it repeatedly against the whetstone. Over time, the word evolved in its meaning, first from the act of sharpening, then to a piercing action, and finally to the process of teaching. The basic idea behind this verse, then, is that by repeating the teachings of the faith, parents will eventually infuse these beliefs into the hearts and minds of their children.

Verse seven continues, "Talk about them when you sit at home and when you walk along the road, when you lie down and when you get up." This is to say, teach your children in every situation in life—morning, noon, and night. When you are at home, teach them. When you are driving to the grocery store, teach them. When you are on vacation, teach them. When you help them say their goodnight prayers, teach them.

Teach your children that God is the Creator. Show them the beauty and intricacies of nature and teach them that it is all by God's design. Teach them about sin, about the difference between right and wrong and how our behavior can distance ourselves from God and from each other. Teach them about Jesus, and how his redemptive love reconciles us to God. Teach them about the active, living Spirit of God that guides and comforts us on life's journey. Teach them about sexual morality, sexual self-control, and to celebrate their sexuality as a God-given gift to be treated honorably. Teach them that death is a natural part of life, but because of the grace of God we can look forward to life in heaven. Talk to them about things such as these when you are sitting at home, or out for a walk, when you go to sleep at night, and when you rise in the morning!

Will your children live devoted and faithful lives as followers of Jesus Christ? That really depends on you.

Shielding the Innocence of Children

Amy's experience is similar to many young people's who use the Internet for fun and communication with their friends. It's become a popular way to socialize. Like Amy, many kids are unaware of the potential dangers online.

At any given moment, there are thousands of sexual predators who want to chat with our children. They work hard to engage kids in conversation, searching for weaknesses while trying to build rapport. Their goal is to gain enough personal information that will allow them to proceed to the next level: either engaging in sexual chat online or over the phone, or meeting in person to engage in sexual activity.

Predators want kids to believe they've found a trusted friend who understands them like their parents cannot. They've often had extensive experience talking with children, and the anonymity of the Internet emboldens them and reinforces their fantasies. They can hide in the darkness of cyberspace. So don't be fooled into thinking that just because you can't see them, they're not out there.

They are prowling around on the Internet in places kids frequent, looking to make a connection with a child, and they know it's only a matter of time before they'll be successful. If they're lucky, they'll even convince her to meet offline. What happens next often makes the news, and the details can be frightening.

Such predators have always known where kids congregate, and now the Internet has opened up a new "playground" for them to frequent. They pass themselves off as teenagers and young adults. Some, trying a more "honest" approach, admit they are grown men and act as supportive father figures to win over a child's trust. One should never underestimate the ability of the predator to gain access to kids. They spend a lot of time analyzing and developing different approaches.

Safety Tips for Kids

Please review these safeguards with your children.

- Never give out personal information about yourself or family (name, address, phone number, email address, or passwords to blogs).

- Never give a stranger a photo of yourself. Let your friends know not to pass out your pictures either. Once a photo is sent out over the Internet, you can never get it back. It can be traded and passed on to others hundreds of times. Remember, a picture identifies who you are. Some predators, having gotten a hold of pictures and general locations of children, have sought them out—sometimes successfully.

Parents need to understand and accept that the Internet can be a very dangerous place. However, they are not helpless to protect their children. They can and should educate themselves, establish some family rules for using the Internet, and start a dialogue with their kids about the very real dangers lurking in cyberspace.

Talking about this subject with your children—especially if they're teenagers—can be difficult. They may believe and act like they know everything. But they don't have the life experience you do, and they still need and depend on you despite their push for independence. It's important to communicate that your reason for the discussion is because you love them and want to protect them. They may still tune you out or argue about any rules you try to implement. But in time they will realize you backed up your declarations of "I love you" with actions.

Being a parent isn't easy. You may have to overcome some of your own fears in order to broach this subject with your kids. But remember: If you don't educate them, there are many on

- Never meet people you've met through the Internet offline. Never! You may think you know them, but you have no idea whether the person they've portrayed themselves to be is who they really are. People lie about age, sex, and other personal factors all the time.

- Never accept emails, pictures, or instant messages from strangers.

- Tell a parent if someone online tries to engage you in sexual chat. Cyber-crime can and should be reported to the police.

- If a friend is threatened or harassed online or tells you she plans on meeting someone offline, tell your parents and hers immediately. Your friend may be upset with you, but that phone call may save her life.

the Internet willing to do it for you. That thought should send any fears you may have packing.

On Blogs and Bullying

A blog is like a personal diary, but it allows others to read what you post (unless it is password-protected). Some people post on their interests, while others keep a daily or weekly journal. Pictures can be included. Often the public (or those invited to view your blog) can comment on what you've posted. Xanga and MySpace are two online services which allow people to set up their own blogs. These sites are extremely popular with teens.

Sometimes teens will use blogs, as well as email and instant messages, to anonymously pick on, intimidate or threaten their peers. This is called "cyber-bullying," and it can cause the victim great emotional distress. Moreover, it's difficult to stop a bully you can't identify.

Safety Tips for Parents

- Know your children's passwords and screen names. Check their online profiles regularly. Make sure they do not reveal any personal information that can lead predators to them.

- If your child has a profile or blog on Xanga, MySpace, or any other site, be sure to check it often. Also make it clear to your child not to include any identifying information. Predators comb these sites for leads.

- If your child has a cell phone, do NOT include wireless (Internet capability) in their service plan. Anything they can access on the computer at home can be accessed through a cell phone with wireless.

Cyberbullies have discovered a new way to use the Internet for sexual exploitation. Its called "cyberblackmail." Teenage boys threaten girls by telling them they will spread bad rumors about them at school unless they take their clothes off and perform sexual acts in front of a video recorder that is attached to the computer. The boy watches 'the show" on his home computer because it is telecast over the Internet. The boy will promise "the show" is private but often forwards the images to other boys who are watching on their computers. The girl often has no clue as to how many of her peers have watched her on the Internet until this information is passed around school. She is exploited and humiliated.

New technology has now been developed by Tribinium Corporation that addresses the limitations of current 'filtering' technology.

"See No Evil™" is a breakthrough software technology that blocks objectionable, pornographic visual content and graphic language while providing access to all Internet websites.

The "See No Evil™" system blocks unknown and objectionable Internet visual content before it can be seen, regardless of its location on the Internet or its inclusion in a list or database. This is accomplished without keeping the user from viewing valid content.

"See No Evil™" is another important weapon to be used in protecting children from exposure to pornography.

IN AMY'S WORDS

When my mom started talking to me about how I needed to make some changes in how I use the Internet, I threw a fit. It wasn't fair that I had to change my screen name and online profile just because some creep tried to talk dirty to me!

However, once I started really listening to what my mom had to say, I began to see things from her point of view. I never realized that people I didn't know—and didn't want to know—could learn so much about me through the Internet. I mean, it's scary when you really think about it.

My mom also doesn't want me going into any chatrooms. I've heard about them from my friends and I didn't think anything was wrong with them. But my mom says that men go into these rooms, sometimes pretending to be teenagers—even girl teenagers! Gross! Some get off just by talking to you, but others are sexual predators who try to befriend you and get you to meet them. Now I know why she doesn't want my personal contact information getting out there.

I know you're not supposed to give out your name, phone number, or address to anyone you don't know, but some of these guys online are really persistent. They'll keep instant-messaging you anytime they see you're online. I now know how to block these creeps, and I've changed my screen name and profile, too. It no longer contains any identifying information.

It was a bit of a hassle to make these changes, and I'm still ticked that there are so many weirdoes in the world who make it necessary. But I know my mom really loves me since she took the time to learn about this stuff and even put up with me yelling at her when she first started talking about it.

Some of my friends don't understand why my parents are so strict about the Internet. I just tell them what my mom and dad have always told me. It's better to be safe than sorry.

WORDS OF WARNING FROM A SEXUAL PREDATOR

I surf the Internet hunting for girls. I prefer girls between the ages of twelve and fifteen. There's something about this age range that drives me crazy. The girls are so cute and innocent.

Many men have the same fantasy. We go to parks, playgrounds, and the mall. We go where the girls go. Sometimes we just watch them. Sometimes we follow them. And sometimes we even strike up a conversation with them.

Some men prefer boys, but girls are my desire. I've taken pictures of them with my digital camera without them suspecting a thing. I make up sexual fantasies about the girls in the pictures and masturbate to them.

Now the Internet has brought many of these girls to my doorstep. It's made my pursuit much easier. There are so many naive girls online! And their parents are even worse! They think that just because their child is on the home computer, she's somehow safe from guys like me.

When I make contact with her, she won't suspect a thing looking at my screen name: DaddyTeddyBear. I have more than one screen name, but I use this one most often. All my screen names project warmth and kindness. It's important that the girls feel safe with me.

My profile also makes me sound like a really nice guy. In it, I describe how I like animals, sunsets, and buying things for girls. Girls like it when you buy them things.

I find most of my conquests by surfing the chatrooms teen girls like to frequent. I read their profiles and then try establishing contact with them in the chatroom or through an instant message. I always start out by asking her how her day is going. Then I'll make a positive comment about something in her profile.

Once she's talking to me, I start the "grooming" process. This is how I get her to trust me. I ask about school, her boyfriend, and her parents. I'm looking for any indication that she's lonely or having problems with her parents. Girls will tell you so much about themselves when they're upset or feeling needy. I give them a shoulder to cry on and convince them that I'm their ally.

If I feel it's safe to ask them questions about their physical appearance, I'll take the risk. I'll say how pretty she must be, or how the boys must be all over her. Then I'll ask her if she's alone. If she is, I'll steer the conversation toward sex. I usually start by asking if her boyfriend is a good kisser. If she responds positively, then I know there's a good chance she'll discuss sexual experiences in greater detail. Hearing about real-life sexual experiences is very arousing. Often, I'll masturbate while she talks.

In time, as I gain her trust, I'll ask if she'll send me a picture of herself. I'll ask if she wants to see me naked. Some girls have said yes. Some have sent naked pictures of themselves in return.

My ultimate goal is to meet these girls offline. I tell them I will buy them something if we meet. I won't pressure them for sex, but my fantasy is they will want to have sex after we meet. I make them promise never to tell anyone about our conversations. I tell them adults, especially parents, won't understand. I tell them how much I value their friendship and want it to continue. I tell them they are special and I want to take care of them. If we meet, we meet in a public place. If they get scared or back out at this point, I simply go back to a chatroom and start all over again.

So I'm curious—do you know who your children talk to online? Can you be sure? I'll promise you this: If you aren't watching over your children, somebody else is. And it may be someone like me.

Creating Order out of Chaos

Recovery from Cybersexual Addiction

LARRY'S STORY

My heart was pounding as it was my turn to speak. All eyes were fixed on me. I took a deep breath, arose from my seat and spoke the words all were waiting to hear, "Hello, I'm Larry and I'm a sex addict." The group members broke into a loud applause and roar of approval.

I recently discovered I have a sexual addiction problem. I go to counseling and attend a twelve-step recovery program called Sexual Addiction Anonymous. This is a support group for men and women who struggle with sexual addiction. It's very similar to alcoholics anonymous. People talk about their problems, support each other, and don't criticize or judge harshly. I feel safe there

I never realized sex could become addictive. I thought all guys liked sex as much as I did. I also never realized many good men, and particularly men of faith shared in similar struggles. This was a very surprising revelation to me, but also comforting to know I was not alone in my struggles.

My journey of discovering I was a sex addict has been a painful one, but there's also a sense of freedom in admitting I have a problem.

My counselor and supportive wife have reassured me that it takes a lot of courage to admit to ones problems. For years, I struggled in silence, keeping my secret all to myself. I was afraid to look at myself in the mirror and admit I had a weakness. Maybe it was pride, or fear that others would look down on me if they knew of my secret. After all, I tried hard to be a good man of faith, but I often felt like a failure. It was like living a double life.

I cared about God and my family, but I could not handle the thought of my wife and children finding out my secrets. My children looked up to me. They put me on a pedestal. My wife trusted me, and I've always tried to set a good Christian example. So deep inside, I knew I was betraying God and my faith. Despite prayers to help me stop, it seemed like lust and sex controlled me. I knew what I was doing was wrong, but there were times I didn't really want to stop. I had made so many promises to stop, but then broke them repeatedly. I reached a point where I was so discouraged; I doubted whether I could really stop at all.

■ ■ ■

My story begins when I was a teenager. This was back in the '70s before computers. I heard about sex and girls at school, as well as playboy magazines. The guys at school talked about finding this type of magazine in their parent's bedroom, usually hidden in a closet or box. So, like a curious boy, I searched my parent's bedroom like a detective on a mission. To my amazement and excitement, I found my first playboy magazine and a book of short stories with sexual themes in my father's dresser. They were hidden under his t-shirts.

I was filled with joy. I felt I had hit the jackpot. I was at that curious age of thirteen and I was overwhelmed by the excitement of seeing naked women. It was a real adrenaline rush. I looked over each page, one by one very carefully. I didn't want to miss anything. The women were so attractive and exposed their breasts in plain view, and they were big ones too. I sensed I was doing something wrong

I could get in trouble for, but the risk was worth it. I put down the magazine, and started to read through my father's book.

The book didn't have any pictures in it, but each chapter described some type of sexual scene. It was very graphic; I'd never read anything like that before. I thought I'd found something very special. I never read a book so fast. When I was all done, I put the material back very carefully, just like the way I found it. I didn't want to get caught. I knew I found something that was exciting, but I also sensed it might be wrong. I listened for the car to pull up in the driveway. I thought about the pictures and stories all day long. I dreamt about the girls in the pictures at bedtime. I couldn't wait until my parents left me alone again. When they did, I went back to the magazine and book. I memorized the pictures and stories.

We were a church family, and it seemed strange that my own father had pornography. I wondered if my mother knew about this. I was confused, but to this day, I never told him what I found. As time went on, I would go back to the drawer and look and read again. I used to wait for my parents to leave, just so I could hunt for more pornography. Every month, a new magazine would appear.

I was sexually excited by all the pictures, and eventually started to masturbate. As my counselor told me, this reinforced my early desires for pornography because masturbation felt so good. And even though I felt guilty, I never told anyone, especially the guys at school. I didn't want to get in trouble, and certainly didn't want them to know I was masturbating. I was afraid I'd be teased to death.

■ ■ ■

Throughout my teen years, I struggled with masturbation and the desire for pornography. I went back to my dad's drawer for years. I never got caught. There were always new magazines to look at. I started to masturbate more and more. It was like a craving that had to be satisfied. When I could not access the magazines, I'd just think of the pictures in my head. These images were so powerful.

When I got older and went to college, I continued to struggle with pornography. I dismissed it as a problem because I told myself all guys looked at pornography and masturbated. I thought it was rather harmless and normal. I did not realize I was forming an addictive pattern to sex. Sexual addiction was not a concept that was talked about in college.

I dated in school, but was somewhat socially insecure and shy. I lacked social confidence. Girls did not find me that attractive and I felt rejected by the most popular and good-looking girls. I wanted to date more, but relationships never seemed to last that long. Even when I was dating, my desire for pornography did not decrease.

■ ■ ■

My struggle with the desire for pornography continued well after I married. I thought I'd have no need for pornography, and I stopped for a while. After a short period of time, my desire came back. I'd buy magazines and videos and hide them from my wife. I suggested we look at pornography together, but she had no interest and became angered. She thought that was a very strange request. I told her I was just kidding. She had no clue how serious my interest in pornography was at the time. I knew she would be upset if she ever found it. I made sure I had a good hiding place where she would never find it. I knew I'd be ashamed if she ever caught me.

There was a dirty bookstore about two miles form where we lived. I started to go there and watch xxx movies in small booths. It was a strange experience. It was dirty, smelly, and sticky on the floors. There were holes in the walls where you could watch someone masturbate. Sometimes, you would see two guys come out of the same booth. I knew what they were doing in there, and despite being grossed out, I went back to the bookstore. It was like being in a secret club. Guys would look at each other. We all knew why we were there. This was a feeling of acceptance. A few men made sexual passes at me, but I resisted them. I always left feeling guilty and dirty and I'd immediately take a shower and wash my clothes. I tried to wash away the guilt.

▮ ▮ ▮

Eventually we moved to a new city out of state, and there were no dirty bookstores around. That problem took care of itself. I was actually relieved.

One day, while renting a normal movie at the local "family" video store, I noticed a door that said "adults only" on it. I peeked in the room and noticed the walls were covered with XXX videos. I thought how could this be? This is a family video store. I walked in and left with an adult movie. When I'd see mothers and their children in the store, I'd always pretend to be looking at normal movies, wait for them to check out first and when the coast was clear, I'd make a dash to the counter to try to get out of there as soon as possible. It was embarrassing to go up to the counter and check out a dirty movie in front of some young kid. Often times the clerk was a girl. I could never look them in the eye. I always paid cash. I worried someone might recognize me. What would I have said? I felt guilty and sleazy and made many promises to stop. I broke each promise and felt more ashamed.

▮ ▮ ▮

My struggle with sexual addiction escalated when we bought a computer and connected to the Internet. I stopped going to the family video store altogether. I found all the pornography I wanted online. This was perfect for me. It was free and anonymous. I no longer had to face the clerk in the video store and risk being seen by someone I knew.

At first, I'd spend countless hours surfing the Internet for pornography. There were places called "galleries." These are pornography sites where pictures are stored and collected. Many sites are organized by theme, e.g., Amateur wives, teens, group sex etc. You just click the theme of interest, and a picture appears on your computer screen. It's that easy and quick.

It's like going to a buffet. The pornographers even refer to it as a "menu." Pictures often appear as "thumbnails." These are very small pick pictures.

You click on the small picture, and it enlarges on the computer screen within seconds. With the speed of the Internet, hundreds of different Web sites and pictures can be viewed during the course of an hour. Many Web sites tempt you with free pictures because they want someone to pay a monthly fee and become a member. A member gets "VIP" status. This means they get a more pictures on a daily and monthly basis than a non-member. There seems to be an endless supply of pictures.

■ ■ ■

The Internet also allows one to view pornographic movies. The faster the computer, the clearer the movie appears. They look like movies one would buy or rent from a store. They tempt one with "trailers." This is a thirty-second sample of a full-length movie that is free. If the sample hooks the individual's interest and desire, the movie can be bought online and downloaded into the computer. The gratification is instant, and pornography movies do not arrive in the mail. It's an easy way to avoid detection.

Some people buy web cams that are like small cameras that attach to the computer. They use the camera to take pictures of themselves and send them to someone who wants to look at the picture. These cameras are very easy to purchase at stores carrying computer equipment. They are very small and easy to hide when one is not using them.

■ ■ ■

As Internet pornography began to lose some excitement, I discovered chatrooms. These are rooms set up by the online service or by members of the service. All chatrooms were identified by themes. I was shocked to see rooms with themes about children and incest. I visited these rooms and watched the sexual conversations about children, but I never talked in those rooms. I found them disgusting. Instead, I started to explore several chatrooms that contained themes about wives. I watched and listened, and when I became comfortable, I began discussing my wife in the chat rooms. Many men traded pictures of their wives with others. I was asked many times to trade pictures of my wife as well. I downloaded pictures of women off the Internet and pretended they were my wife and traded them. It was like a trading club. Some wanted to engage in "private" conversations and discuss their fantasies. Many fantasies included watching ones wife in some type of sexual act with another man. Men referred to this activity as "trading" or "sharing."

I found a chatroom entitled "offline chat about wives." I was curious and visited the room. I was instantly hooked on this chatroom. Men found other men to trade pictures and start a sexual conversation about a fantasy of their wives. This progressed to discussing the fantasy by talking about it on the telephone. I tried "phone sex" with several men but I never gave anyone my home or work phone number. There were many men willing to share their numbers so it was easy to find someone to chat with. I bought a phone card at the local gas station and used this to call men. The conversations would turn sexual very quickly. Both parties engaged in masturbation at the same time. When one or both reached orgasm, the phone call usually ended abruptly. I always felt ashamed and dirty after each call. I made several promises to quit, but broke they each time. At the pinnacle of my addiction, I was looking at pornography every day and had phone sex once a week.

■ ■ ■

One night when my wife had fallen asleep on the sofa downstairs, I went upstairs to surf the Internet for pornography and sexual chat. The house was quiet and the children were asleep. I thought I was safe to go online. In the middle of a sexual conversation with a man, I had a pornographic image of a woman enlarged on my computer screen. My wife walked into the bedroom and caught me masturbating. She was shocked and angry. We had a long talk that night and I broke down and told her of my struggles with pornography.

When she calmed down, she suggested I call our pastor the next day. I called him first thing in the morning and met him to discuss this issue. He recognized I had a sexual addiction problem and referred me to a specialist who treated these problems. It was a very, very embarrassing meeting, but I disclosed the truth. I wound up going to counseling and a 12-step support group for sexual addicts. It was a turning point in my life. I made a commitment to get this problem under control. It has been a challenging road to recovery, and although there have been times when I have slipped up and looked at pornography again, I worked hard to get the problem under control. My life was chaos and I was drifting more into the dark side of sexual addiction. Thank goodness my pastor was willing to talk to me openly about my problem and help me get back on the right path.

The Chaos of Sexual Addiction

Larry is a sex addict. This means he developed a psychological dependency on sex e.g. Internet pornography. Larry's case is important to understand because it demonstrates how curiosity about pornography can escalate into an addictive pattern and become a destructive habit over time. Some become addicted within weeks while others progress over months. Every ones pattern is unique to the individual.

Larry was once an innocent little boy who knew nothing about sexuality and the dangers of pornography. The seeds of his addiction were unknowingly planted by his father. He discovered by accident his father's pornography. Imagine how Larry's life journey might have been different if his father had not used pornography.

Instead of keeping his youthful innocence, Larry began to crave pornography and the feelings of arousal and pleasure associated with it. Like alcoholics crave their drug, Larry craved pornography.

Larry was socially insecure as a child and teen. Pornography filled a void in his life. It made him feel good. It helped him cope with social anxiety and the fear of rejection. He used sex to cope with problems and stress in his adult life. Like many addicts, pornography became his crutch. It was his shameful secret.

Larry's addiction continued after marriage. For many addicts, they hope marriage will be the solution to this problem because of the availability of sex. Sometimes this can help, and the addiction lays dormant for a while. In other cases, the addict "brings the addiction" into the marriage and learns to hide it from their spouse rather than confront the problem.

Larry was afraid of exposing his secret life. He feared social criticism and judgment. He hid behind the anonymity of the computer. When he became bored with pornography, he found chatrooms. This was an exciting discovery. He justified his actions and his addiction escalated. When caught by his wife, the walls hiding his addiction came tumbling down. The secret was out of the bag. It was time to look into the mirror and face reality.

Larry's story is also one of strength and courage. It takes courage to admit when one has a problem and face it directly. He was willing to share his story with others. Larry went to counseling, found a twelve step-recovery support group and sought spiritual guidance from his pastor. These were necessary steps for recovery to take place. He took the first step by admitting he had a problem. This courageous first step led to a journey of exploration and healing. Larry's new motto: "No more secrets."

The Cycle of Sexual Addiction

Patrick Carnes played an instrumental role in advocating for the concept of sexual addiction as a recognizable and treatable problem. He authored the book entitled *Out of the Shadows* in the 1980s, which discussed sexual addiction.[2] He went on to author additional books which helped to explain the complexities of sexual addiction.

Carnes believed that sex could become an addiction for some people, just as drugs and alcohol become an addiction for other people. Like other addictions, sexual addiction bears four hallmarks: It builds tolerance. It produces withdrawal. It follows obsessive-compulsive patterns. And, finally, sexual addiction produces shame.

Moreover, Carnes determined six warning signs for people to look for in order to determine whether sex has become

What Is Sexual Addiction?

Several conceptual models have been developed to understand sexual addiction. Mark Griffiths[1] identified six core components of addiction, including:

Salience. *Salience* occurs when Internet sex becomes the most important activity in the person's life and dominates their thinking (preoccupations and cognitive distortions), feelings (cravings), and behavior (deterioration of socialized behavior). For instance, even if the person is not actually on their computer engaged in Internet sex they will be thinking about the next time they will be.

Mood modification. *Mood modification* refers to the subjective experience (an arousing "buzz" or "high" or paradoxically tranquilizing feeling of "escape" or "numbing") that people report having as a consequence of engaging in Internet sex. It is often viewed as coping strategy.

Tolerance. *Tolerance* is the process whereby increasing amounts of Internet sex are required to achieve the former mood an addiction. Addictive sex is done in isolation. Addictive sex is secretive. It is devoid of intimacy. It is devoid of relationship. It is victimizing. And addictive sex always ends in despair.

As Carnes studied sexual addiction, he noted that it progressed through four levels. In level one, the addict uses fantasy, pornography, and masturbation to achieve a high (that is, sexual release). In level two, the addict needs live pornography to provide release. He also may develop a fetish and seek sex outside of marriage to feed his high.

By level three, the addict's growing drive may lead to minor criminal offenses, prostitution, voyeurism, and/or exhibitionism. If he does not seek help at this point for his addiction, he

modifications effects. This basically means that for someone engaged in Internet sex, they gradually build up the amount of the time they spend on front of the computer engaged in the behavior.

Withdrawal. *Withdrawal* symptoms are the unpleasant feeling states and/or physical effects which occur when Internet sex is discontinued or suddenly reduced (e.g., the shakes, moodiness, irritability, etc.).

Conflict. *Conflict* refers to the conflicts between the Internet user and those around them (interpersonal conflict), conflicts with other activities (job, social life, hobbies, and interests), or conflicts within themselves (intrapsychic conflict and/or subjective feelings of loss of control), which are concerned with spending too much time engaged in Internet sex.

Relapse. *Relapse* is the tendency for repeated reversions to earlier patterns of Internet sex to recur and for even the most extreme patterns typical of the height of excessive Internet sex to be quickly restored after many years of abstinence or control.

will progress to level four and face severe legal consequences for molestation, incest, and/or rape.

Carnes used these words to describe the cycle of sexual addiction: *obsession, the hunt, recruitment, gratification, return to normal, justification, blame, shame, despair, and promises.*

Support Groups for Sexual Addicts

The 1980s gave birth to the support group movement as a way to acknowledge and combat sexual addiction. This included using a twelve-step recovery model very similar to Alcoholics Anonymous. Group members referred to as "recovering addicts" established support groups in communities and followed the twelve-step philosophy. Group members including men and women shared stories of success and struggles, and encouraged others to share in an open and non-judgmental environment. Groups were not run or managed by therapists or counselors. Group members are encouraged to take responsibility for addictive behavior and recognize the value relying on others and a "higher power" for fellowship and strength.

The higher power is usually associated with some belief and perception of God, but not affiliated with a specific denomination or faith community.

Sexaholics Anonymous (SA), Sexual Compulsive Anonymous (SCA), and Sex and Love Addicts Anonymous (SALA) are popular recovery programs for sexual addiction.[3] Each organization has a Web site that identifies their philosophy of recovery, informational material on sexual addiction, and contact numbers.

The Twelve-Step Model

An example of the Sexual Compulsive Anonymous twelve-step model identifies the following steps:

> 1. We admitted we were powerless over the sexual compulsion-that our lives had become unmanageable.

2. Came to believe that a Power greater than ourselves could restore us to sanity.

3. Made a decision to turn our will and our lives over to the care of God as we understood God.

4. Made a searching and fearless moral inventory of ourselves.

5. Admitted to God, to ourselves and to another human being the exact nature of our wrongs.

6. Were entirely ready to have God remove all these defects of character.

7. Humbly asked God to remove our shortcomings.

8. Made a list of all persons we had harmed, and became willing to make amends to them all.

9. Made a direct amends to such people wherever possible, except when to do so would injure them or others.

10. Continued to take personal inventory, and when we were wrong promptly admitted it.

11. Sought through prayer and meditation to improve our conscious contact with God as we understood God, praying only for knowledge of God's will for us and the power to carry that out.

12. Having had a spiritual awakening as the result of these steps, we tried to carry this message to sexually compulsive people and to practice these principles in all our affairs.

Celebration Recovery

Pastor Rick Warren, author of the widely popular The Purpose Drive Life, began a "Celebrate Recovery" ministry through his Saddleback Church in California.[4] The founder of the program is Pastor John Baker. This program identifies Jesus Christ as the specific and only Higher Power. This program can be used to help those addicted to sex. It outlines eight key recovery principles based on the Beatitudes. These principles include the following:

R= Realize I'm not God; I admit that I am powerless to control my tendency to do the wrong thing and my life is unmanageable

E= Earnestly that God exists, that I matter to him, and that he has the power to help me recover.

C= Consciously choose to commit all my life and will to Christ's care and control.

O=Openly examine and confess my faults to God, to myself, and to someone I trust.

V= Voluntarily submit to every change God wants to make in my life and humbly ask Him to remove my character defects.

E= Evaluate all my relationships; Offer forgiveness to those who have hurt me and make amends for harm I've done to others except when to do so would harm them or others.

R= Reserve a daily time for God for self examination, Bible readings and prayer in order to know God and His will for my life and to gain the power to follow is will.

Y= Yield myself to God to be used to bring his Good News to others, both by my example and by my words.

Scriptural Guidance for Recovery

In the beginning God created the heavens and the earth. Now the earth was formless and empty, darkness was over the surface of the deep, and the Spirit of God was hovering over the waters. And God said, "Let there be light," and there was light. God saw that the light was good and He separated the light from the darkness. God called the light "day," and the darkness he called "night." And there was evening, and there was morning-the first day.

And God said, "Let there be an expanse between the waters to separate water from the water." God made the expanse and separated the water under the expanse from the water above it. And it was so. God called the expanse "sky." And there was evening, and there was morning-the second day.

And God said, "Let the water under the sky be gathered to one place, and let dry ground appear." And it was so. God called the dry ground "land," and the gathered waters he called "seas." And God saw that it was good. Then God said, "Let the land produce vegetation: seed-bearing plants and trees on the land that bear fruit with seed in it, according to their various kinds." And it was so. The land produced vegetation: plants bearing seed according to their kinds and trees bearing fruit with seed in it according to their kinds. And God saw that it was good. And there was evening, and there was morning-the third day.

And God said, "Let there be lights in the expanse of the sky to separate the day from the night, and let them serve as signs to mark seasons and days and years, and let them be lights in the expanse of the sky to give light on the earth." And it was so. God made two great lights-the greater light to govern the day and the lesser light to govern the night. He also made the stars. God set them in the expanse of the sky to give light on the earth, to govern the day and the night, and to separate light from darkness. And God saw that it was good. And there was evening. And there was morning-the fourth day.

And God said, "Let the water teem with living creatures, and let birds fly above the earth across the expanse of the sky." So God created the great creatures of the sea and every living and moving thing with which the water teems, according to their kinds, and every winged bird according to its kind. And God saw that it was good. God blessed them and said, "Be fruitful and increase in number and fill the water in the seas, and let the birds increase on the earth." And there was evening, and there was morning-the fifth day.

And God said, "Let the land produce living creatures according to their kinds: livestock, creatures that move along the ground, and wild animals, each according to its kind." And it was so. God made the wild animals according to t heir kinds, the livestock according to their kinds, and all the creatures that move along the ground according to their kinds. And God saw that it was good. Then God said, "Let us make man in our image, in our likeness, and let them rule over the fish of the sea and the birds of the air, over the livestock, over all the earth, and over all the creatures that move along the ground." So God created man in his own image, in the image of God he created him; male and female he created them. God blessed them and said to them. "Be fruitful and increase in number; fill the earth and subdue it. Rule over the fish of the sea and the birds of the air and over every living creature that moves on the ground." Then God said, "I give you every seed-bearing plant on the face of the whole earth and every tree that has fruit with seed in it. They will be yours for food. And to all the beasts of the earth and all the birds of the air and all the creatures that move on the ground-everything that has the breath of life in it-I give every green plant for food." And it was so. God saw all that he had made, and it was very good. And there was evening, and there was morning-the sixth day.

Thus the heavens and the earth were completed in all their vast array. By the seventh day God had finished *the work he had been doing; so on the seventh day he rested from all his work. And God blessed the seventh day and made it holy. because on it rested from all the work of creating that he had done."*

GENESIS 1:1—2:3, NIV

Naomi Rosenblatt and Joshua Horwitz, authors of *Wrestling With Angels: What Genesis Teaches Us About Our Spiritual Identity, Sexuality, and Personal Relationships,* write:

In his first creative burst, God displays all the loving concern of an ideal parent as He prepares the world for humanity's arrival. Establishing basic boundaries or order and predictability, He begins to build the safe and secure infrastructure that every infant must have to establish trust in her world. A child learns to trust through predictability and routine. As psychologist Erik Erikson pointed out, a newborn baby first learns trust through her own bodily systems. As she begins to breathe and sleep and digest her mother's milk, the predictable functioning of her body becomes an analogue of the rhythms of the outside world – the days, the seasons, the tides. Day by day the child grows to trust in these consistent patterns in her life. Over time she begins to smile in recognition of the benignly predictable world around her.

To fulfill our potential as human beings we all need a modicum of order in our physical environment. The first thing a social worker tries to create in a troubled child's home is order and routine. Without a few fixed points in his daily life—dinnertime, bedtime, a parent at the breakfast table or waiting when he comes home from school—a child can't trust and learn and grow. Neither can an adult.

In the first day of creation, God creates order out of chaos. He creates light to balance the darkness. And he creates time by establishing a predictable progression from darkness to light, from evening to morning. This simple fact of life on earth—— that the planet rotates regularly on its axis, that after every midnight there will be a dawn—gives order and stability to both our physical and spiritual existence. Every child who is frightened of the dark clings to this predictable truth. A Hebrew morning prayer praises God as "the One who renews creation every day." Each day's dawn renews our connection to the Creator and offers us the promise of a new beginning.[5]

Cybersexual addiction leads to personal and family chaos. There are very real consequences for straying from God's plan and purpose. When a person is addicted to sex, their entire spiritual life spins out of control. But there is hope. God continues to create order out of chaos.

Read through the verses written above from the book of Genesis. As you read, notice the pattern within the verses. Notice how the ancient writers used repetition to emphasize and punctuate the beauty of the process of creation. Notice how on each day of creation it is written, "And there was evening, and there was morning—the first day." And the second day. And the third and the fourth, the fifth, and the sixth. With each stage of creating order out of chaos it is proclaimed that it was a day, and that it was good. But notice the absence of such repetition for the seventh day.

Could it be that the ancient writers were helping us to understand that God continues to be involved in our world? That God continues to participate in your life? That God continues to work with you to help create order out of your chaos?

The story of creation does indeed demonstrate how God created order out of chaos. And that creative, redemptive power is still available to those who believe in Him.

Strategies for Recovery and Change

The first step in healing and recovery is to admit one has a problem. This can also be the most difficult step to take. Shame and embarrassment, lack of understanding and awareness of the destructive nature of cyber sexual behavior, and resistance to break the addiction pattern because of pleasure keep many from taking this important step toward change. Admission of a problem takes courage and builds character. It results in taking responsibility for ones actions. People are more likely to change when they recognize a problem and are motivated to fix it. The stronger the motivation the better.

Changing old habits or patterns which have been around for a long time is hard work. There can be self-doubt, a tendency to give up easily and fear of failure. It can be easy to give up in the face of adversity. It is often a daily battle and often times there are relapses. The craving to satisfy sexual desire is powerful and intoxicating. Fortunately, there is a way to attack this problem and win the battle. Larry's case illustrates the keys to victory.

Developing a Game Plan

Prayer

Larry was encouraged to pray on a daily basis for healing and spiritual renewal. This included praying every time he felt the desire to sexually act out. He was comforted to know he had a powerful weapon at his disposal. He learned prayer worked and began a prayer routine. He started and ended each day with prayer and personal reflection. This helped get the day off to a good start and relax before bedtime. It gave him confidence that he could face any temptation that would come his way.

Spiritual Guidance

Larry sought spiritual guidance from his pastor. This included reading daily devotions and other material designed to grow his spiritual life. He followed his pastor's advice and contacted a Christian counselor who was experienced in treating sexual addiction. Larry became more active in the church and joined a men's Bible and prayer support group. He was supported and encouraged by a powerful team of believers.

Counseling

Larry followed his pastor's advice and went to counseling. This was a very big step for Larry. He always believed he could solve his own problems and usually kept his inner most thoughts and feelings to himself. He was nervous at first, but once rapport and trust was established with his counselor, he began to relax. The counselor explained the purpose of counseling was to talk about and understand, in as much depth as possible Larry's addiction to pornography. The counselor explained Larry would develop tools for controlling these desires. Larry began to feel confident and hoped he could change. Larry talked openly and honestly about his life. Talking about personal issues was hard work and at times emotionally painful; however, Larry realized the power of expressing himself. He admitted he was afraid of opening up old emotional wounds from his past. He had a great deal of hurt and pain, but over time he began to feel better.

Larry learned how his curiosity about pornography escalated over time into a habit and addiction. He then focused on identifying all the possible triggers in his life (personal and situational) that made him want to engage in cyber sexual behavior. He discovered stress was a major trigger. Financial and work pressures were the top situational stressors. He worried about whether he could adequately provide for his family and whether or not he will still have the same job in the next few years. He learned more effective ways of recognizing and coping with his stress e.g. talking about what bothered him as opposed to bottling up his feelings and lashing out at him in anger. Once he became more skilled at recognizing early warning signs to mounting stress levels, he reacted more quickly to gain control of it. He was learning a new way of coping rather than using cyber sexual behavior as a crutch.

Larry took a break from the computer. He stopped using the computer altogether for a while and removed it as a temptation. Sometimes this is difficult to do for those who need the computer for work. Under these conditions, it is extremely important to have an accountability partner and use computer software that will let your accountability partner know if you have visited

Ten Keys to Successful Counseling

1. Find a Christian counselor with some expertise in the field of sexual addiction.

2. Trust the counselor for guidance and advice.

3. Have a positive attitude about getting help.

4. Be motivated to change and sustain the motivation over time.

5. Tell the truth. If one is tempted to relapse or has relapsed, tell the counselor.

6. Follow through on homework assignments. They are given for a purpose and are designed to facilitate change.

7. Insight and self-awareness can be invaluable tools as long as they are used and applied on a daily basis.

8. Practice techniques and interventions.

9. Strengthen the marriage and family.

10. Work hard to grow in one's spiritual faith.

a pornography Web site. Another option is to install software that blocks pornographic images altogether.

Larry followed the motto of taking one day at a time. Every good day counts as a victory. Every temptation that is resisted is a victory. There will be many temptations to relapse, but these are opportunities for change and success. Every desire to turn on the computer and look at pornography that is thwarted is a win. Each win is a building block toward personal growth and maturity. Over time, one's character will change in a positive way and the desire to use pornography will decrease.

Larry also attended a support designed to assist men and women in recovery from sexual issues. He found the support of the group to be very helpful. He was able to learn from others experiences and realized he was not alone in his suffering. He was very nervous and embarrassed, but overcame his insecurities and shared openly about his struggles with pornography.

A WORD FROM LARRY'S PASTOR

Larry came to me a broken man. When he told me he had a problem with Internet pornography, we immediately prayed for forgiveness and healing. I referred Larry to a counselor I knew who dealt with this kind of problem. His counselor confirmed Larry had an addiction to pornography and began to develop a treatment plan for him. I, along with a group of men from our church, became Larry's accountability and prayer partners. Together, we helped Larry refocus his spirituality. This proved invaluable to Larry's recovery.

Notes

Chapter 1

1. Alexa Research. (2001). *Alexa Research finds "sex" popular on web.* Business Wire, February 14, 2001.

2. Cooper, A., Delmonico, D., & Burg, R. (2000). Cybersex users, abusers, and compulsives: New findings and implications. In A. Cooper (Ed.), *Cybersex: The dark side of the force* (pp. 5-29). Philadelphia: Brunner-Routledge.

3. Focus on the Family. (2000). *Zogby survey reveals a growing percentage of those seeking sexual fulfillment on the Internet.* Retrieved March 1, 2003 from the World Wide Web: www.pureintimacy.org/news/a0000031.html

4. Ropelato, Jerry (2007). *Internet Pornography Statistics.* Internet Filter Review. Retrieved from the Wold Wide Web on July 31, 2007: http://internet-filter-review.toptenreviews.com/internet-pornography-statistics.html

5. Cited in: *Archive of Statistics on Internet Dangers*, Enough Is Enough, Retrieved from the World Wide Web on July 31, 2007 at www.enough.org/inside.php?tag=stat%20archives

Chapter 2

1. Stanford/Duquesne. (2000). *Extent of the problem.* Retrieved, from the World Wide Web: www.familyschoice.com/main/extent-stats.htm

2. Cited in: *Archive of Statistics on Internet Dangers*, Enough Is Enough, Retrieved from the World Wide Web on July 31, 2007 at www.enough.org/inside.php?tag=stat%20archives

3. Ropelato, Jerry (2007). *Internet Pornography Statistics.* Internet Filter Review. Retrieved from the Wold Wide Web on July 31, 2007: http://internet-filter-review.toptenreviews.com/internet-pornography-statistics.html

4. Cooper, A., (2000). Cybersex users, abusers, and compulsives: New findings and implications. In A. Cooper (Ed.), *Cybersex: The dark side of the force* (pp. 5-29). Philadelphia: Brunner-Routledge.

5. Grundner, Tom ((2000). The Skinner Box Effect. Lincoln, Nebraska: Writers Club Press.

Chapter 3

1. Steketee, Gail; Pigott, Teresa; and Schemmel, Todd (2003). Obsessive Compulsive Disorder: The Latest Assessment and Treatment Strategies. Kansas City, MO: Compact Clinicals.

Chapter 4

1. Cooper, A., (2000). Cybersex users, abusers, and compulsives: New findings and implications. In A. Cooper (Ed.), *Cybersex: The dark side of the force* (pp. 5-29). Philadelphia: Brunner-Routledge.

2. Schneider, J. P. (2000). Effects of cybersex addiction on the family: Results from a survey. In A. Cooper (Ed.), *Cybersex: The Dark Side of the Force* (pp. 31-58). Philadelphia: Brunner-Routledge.

3. Quittner, J. (April 14, 1997). Divorce Internet style. *Time*, 72.

4. Smedes, Lewis (1984). Forgive and Forget: Healing the Wounds We Don't Deserve. San Francisco, CA: Harper San Francisco.

5. Ibid.

6. Flanigan, Beverly

7. Adapted from Flanigan's model of reciprocal forgiveness and reconciliation.

8. National Institute of Mental Health (2007). *Depression.* Retrieved from the World Wide Web on August 15, 2007: http://

www.nimh.nih.gov/healthinformation/depressionmenu.cfm

Chapter 5

1. Sharf, Richard S. (1996). Theories of Psychotherapy and Counseling: Concepts and Cases. Pacific Grove, CA: Brooks/Cole Publishing Company.

2. Cooper, A., Delmonico, D., & Burg, R. (2000). Cybersex users, abusers, and compulsives: New findings and implications. In A. Cooper (Ed.), *Cybersex: The dark side of the force* (pp. 5-29). Philadelphia: Brunner-Routledge.

3. Schneider, J. P. (2000). Effects of cybersex addiction on the family: Results from a survey. In A. Cooper (Ed.), *Cybersex: The Dark Side of the Force* (pp. 31-58). Philadelphia: Brunner-Routledge.

4. Ibid: Sharf, Richard S.

Chapter 7

1. Whealin, J. (n.d.). Child Sexual Abuse. National Center for PTSD Fact Sheet. Retrieved from the World Wide Web on March 26, 2006: http://www.ncptsd.va.gov/ncmain/ncdocs/fact_shts/fs_child_sexual_abuse.html?opm=1&rr=rr1747&srt=d&echorr=true

2. Kraizer, S. (1996). Sexual Abuse. The Safe Child Program. Retrieved from the World Wide Web on March 21, 2006: http://safechild.org/childabuse1.htm#Indicators%20of%20Sexually%20Abusive%20Parent/Guardian

3. Darkness to Light (2007) *Statistics Surrounding Child Sexual Abuse*. Retrieved from the World Wide Web on August 27, 2007: www.darkness2light.org/KnowAbout

Chapter 8

1. Operation Innocence Online (2006). Retrieved from the World Wide Web on June 26, 2006: http://innocenceonline.com/statistics-main.asp

2. Frank Stanley can be contacted at: Frank Stanley, P.C., Attorney At Law, 200 North Division Avenue, Grand Rapids, Michigan 48503

Chapter 9

1. Operation Innocence Online (2006). Retrieved from the World Wide Web on June 26, 2006: http://innocenceonline.com/statistics-main.asp

Chapter 10

1. Griffiths, Mark (2000). *Does Internet and Computer "Addiction" Exist? Some Case Study Evidence*. Cyberpsychology & Behavior, 3(2): 211-218.

2. Carnes, P. (1983). *Out of the shadows: Understanding Sexual Addiction*. Minneapolis, Minn: Compcare.

3. For more information about these recovery support groups, go to: www.sa.org , www.sca-recovery.org, and www.slaafws.org

4. For more information go to: www.celebrationrecovery.com

5. Rosenblatt, Naomi, and Horwitz, Joshua. (1995). Wrestling With Angels. New York: Delacorte Press.